First World War
and Army of Occupation
War Diary
France, Belgium and Germany

5 CAVALRY DIVISION
Divisional Troops
5 (Cavalry) Sanitary Section
1 January 1917 - 30 April 1918

WO95/1163/7

The Naval & Military Press Ltd
www.nmarchive.com
Published in association with The National Archives

Published by

The Naval & Military Press Ltd

Unit 10 Ridgewood Industrial Park,

Uckfield, East Sussex,

TN22 5QE England

Tel: +44 (0) 1825 749494

www.naval-military-press.com

www.nmarchive.com

This diary has been reprinted in facsimile from the original. Any imperfections are inevitably reproduced and the quality may fall short of modern type and cartographic standards.

© Crown Copyright
Images reproduced by permission of The National Archives, London, England, 2015.

Contents

Document type	Place/Title	Date From	Date To
Heading	WO95/1163/7		
Heading	5th Sanitary Section Jan 1917-Jan 1918		
Heading	War Diary of Sanitary Section, 5th Cavalry Division. From 1st January 1917 To 31st January 1917		
War Diary	Bouvaincourt	01/01/1917	31/01/1917
Heading	No 5 (Cav) San. Sect. Feb 1917		
War Diary	Bouvaincourt	01/02/1917	28/02/1917
Heading	Sanitary Section, 5th Cav Div. Feb 1917		
Heading	Sanitary Section, 5th Cavalry Division. From 1st to 28th February 1917		
War Diary	Bouvaincourt	01/02/1917	28/02/1917
Heading	Sanitary Section-5th Cav Div April 1917		
War Diary	Villers-Bretonneux	01/04/1917	13/04/1917
War Diary	Guizancourt	14/04/1917	30/04/1917
Heading	No. 5 (Cav.) (San Sect) April 1917		
Miscellaneous	Sanitary Section 5th Cav. Div. for month ending 30.4.17		
War Diary	Villers-Bretonneux	01/04/1917	13/04/1917
War Diary	Guizancourt	14/04/1917	30/04/1917
Heading	Sanitary Section-5th Cav. Div. Mar 1917		
War Diary	Bouvaincourt.	01/03/1917	20/03/1917
War Diary	Revelles	21/03/1917	21/03/1917
War Diary	Cachy	22/03/1917	23/03/1917
War Diary	Near Herbecourt	24/03/1917	24/03/1917
War Diary	Herbecourt	25/03/1917	27/03/1917
War Diary	Herbecourt	28/03/1917	28/03/1917
War Diary	Camp No East of Cappy	29/03/1917	31/03/1917
Heading	Sanitary Section, 5th Cavalry Division. From 1st may to 30th June 1917		
Heading	Sanitary Section-5th Cav. Div. May to June 1917		
War Diary	Guizancourt	01/05/1917	14/05/1917
War Diary	Camp at Q. 1to 8 9 (62C 1/40000)	15/05/1917	23/05/1917
War Diary	K. 32 b. 4 1 (62c 1/40000)	24/05/1917	31/05/1917
War Diary	Camp near Nobescourt Farm. (map 62c K3 2 b 4 1)	01/06/1917	30/06/1917
Heading	No. 5 (Cav.) San. Sect. May 1917		
War Diary	Guizancourt	01/05/1917	14/05/1917
War Diary	Camp at Q. 1 b 8 9 (62c 1/40000)	15/05/1917	23/05/1917
War Diary	K. 32 b. 4 1 (62c 1/40000)	24/05/1917	31/05/1917
Heading	San. Sect-5th Inf Cav. Div. July 1917		
Heading	5th Cavalry Sanitary Section. From 1st to 31st July 1917		
War Diary	Camp near Nobescourt Farm. K 32 b. 4 1 (map 62c 1/40000)	01/07/1917	09/07/1917
War Diary	Bouvincourt	10/07/1917	15/07/1917
War Diary	St Pol	16/07/1917	31/07/1917
Heading	6th Ind. Cav. Div. San. Sect. Aug 1917		
Heading	5th Cavalry Sanitary Section. From 1st to 31st August 1917		
War Diary	St Pol	01/08/1917	31/08/1917
Heading	5th Cav. Div. Sanitary Section Sept 1917		
War Diary	St Pol	01/09/1917	30/09/1917

Type	Location	From	To
Heading	5th Cav. Sanitary Section. Oct 1917		
War Diary	St Pol	01/10/1917	05/10/1917
War Diary	Camp South of Steenbecque Station	06/10/1917	07/10/1917
War Diary	Watou	08/10/1917	14/10/1917
War Diary	Leauwette	15/10/1917	16/10/1917
War Diary	La Loge	17/10/1917	31/10/1917
Heading	5th Cav. Sanitary Sections. Nov 1917		
War Diary	La Loge	01/11/1917	10/11/1917
War Diary	Quinconce (Peronne)	11/11/1917	23/11/1917
War Diary	Proyart	24/11/1917	27/11/1917
War Diary	Monchy-Lagache	28/11/1917	30/11/1917
Heading	5th Cav. San. Sect. Dec 1917		
War Diary	Athies	01/12/1917	02/12/1917
War Diary	V. 8 Central (1/40000) 62c)	03/12/1917	17/12/1917
War Diary	Monchy-Lagache	18/12/1917	30/01/1918
War Diary	Domart-En-Ponthieu	31/01/1918	31/01/1918
Heading	No. 5 San. Sect. Mar 1918		
War Diary	Troop train M.E.D. No 696 H.V.S	01/03/1918	11/03/1918
War Diary	Hitleasowe Castle	12/03/1918	20/03/1918
War Diary	Camp Tel-El-Kebir	21/03/1918	31/03/1918
Heading	No. 5 (Cav) San. Sect. April 1918		
War Diary	Camp Tel-El-Kebir	01/04/1918	30/04/1918

WO 95/1163/7

1917-1918
5TH CAVALRY DIVISION

5TH SANITARY SECTION
JAN 1917 - JAN 1918

Jan. 1917

SERIAL NO. 297.

Confidential War Diary of

SANITARY SECTION, 5th CAVALRY DIVISION.

COMMITTEE FOR THE
MEDICAL HISTORY OF THE WAR
Date 23 APR. 1917

FROM 1st January 1917 _191_ TO 31st January 1917 _191_

Volume XX

WAR DIARY or INTELLIGENCE SUMMARY.

Army Form C. 2118.

No 5 (Cav.) Sanitary Section

Place	Date	Hour	Summary of Events and Information	Remarks and references to Appendices
BdCLAINCOURT	1st Jan. 1917		1 Indian N.C.O and 6 men detached to R.S.O. Duties changed at Divisional school + D.H.Q.	
	2nd Jan		1 Br N.C.O. and 6 sweepers detached with Amballa Pioneer Battalion.	
"	"		Party of 1 N.C.O and 8 men worked at BEUCHAMPS for Aux H.T.	
	3rd Jan		Party of 1 N.C.O and 8 men to clean up the road & ground the ration stand G.H.Q.	
"	"		8 sweepers returned from the digging party. See Pioneer Battalion.	
	4th Jan		Sent 1 N.C.O and 8 men with motor lorry to Div gas school AULT.	
	5th Jan		1 N.C.O and 9 men sent to Div school at AULT.	
			1 Ind. N.C.O and 8 men detached to Aux. H.T. at WOUVAINCOURT.	
	6th Jan		Party of 1 N.C.O and 8 men sent to Amballa P.Q.	
			Party of 1. N.C.O and 6 men to D.H.Q. for latrines.	
	8th Jan		1 Br N.C.O and 13 men sent to Div school Ault.	
	9th Jan		1 N.C.O and 8 men sent to D.H.Q.	
	10th Jan		1 N.C.O and 13 men sent to A.H.T. WOINCOURT.	
	11th Jan		1 N.C.O and 2 men to No 1 Mess D.H.Q.	
			1 N.C.O and 12 men sent to A.H.T. WOINCOURT.	
	12th Jan		Handed over charge to Capt Lee. D.M.S.	
				Cameron Lt Ims

WAR DIARY or **INTELLIGENCE SUMMARY.**

N° 5 (Cav.) Sanitary Section

Army Form C. 2118.

Place	Date	Hour	Summary of Events and Information	Remarks and references to Appendices
BOUVAINCOURT	13th Jan. 1917		Parties at GAMACHES (Ambala Br. H.Q.) and Woincourt (Auxiliary Horse Transport)	
"	14/1/17		Inspected W.Cs. and drains at DARGNIES chateau: recommended two to be closed.	
"	15/1/17		Party at WOINCOURT (A.H.Tr.) Foden at LONGROY, 18th Lancers.	
"	16th		Party " " " . Foden at BOUVAINCOURT, 141st C.F.A. and Disl. Hospital.	
"	17th		Party " " " . Foden at BOUVAINCOURT, 141st and 104th C.F.A. horse blankets + jhools.	
"	18th		Party " " " . Foden at FEUQUIERES, 7th Dragoon Guards.	
"	19th + 20th		Party " " " . Foden at TULLY, Canadian Cav. Brigade. Inspected and reported on sanitary and hygienic condition of German Prisoners of War Camp near YZENGREMER.	
"	21st		Foden at German prisoners' camp near YZENGREMER.	
"	22nd and 23rd		Party at WOINCOURT (A.H.Tr.) Foden at INCHEVILLE, working under orders of A.D.V.S.	
"	24th		Party " " " . Foden at TILLOY, working under orders of A.D.V.S. (anti-mange)	
"	25th		Kit inspection. Foden nil, no coal. Reported at Foden requires 400 lb. coal, instead of 200 lb. allowed.	
"	26th		Party at WOINCOURT (A.H.Tr.). Foden nil, no coal.	
"	27th		Party " " " . Coal allowances for Foden increased to 400 lb. per day. Foden at HOCQUELUS, 7th D.G⁰.	
"	28th		Foden at German prisoners camp near YZENGREMER.	
"	29th		Party at WOINCOURT. Foden at FEUQUIERES, 7th D.G⁰.	
"	30th + 31st		Party at WOINCOURT. Erected 2-seated latrine at N°1 mess, DARGNIES.	

R.H.Lee Capt/RAMC
O.C. N° 5 (Cav.) Sanitary Section

Feb 1917.

No 5 (Cav.) San. Sect.

WAR DIARY or INTELLIGENCE SUMMARY.

Army Form C. 2118.

N° 5 (Cav.) Sanitary Section

Place	Date	Hour	Summary of Events and Information	Remarks and references to Appendices
BOUVAINCOURT	1st Feb. 1917		Party at WOINCOURT making horse lines for Auxiliary Horse Transport S.?	
"	2nd and 3rd		Ditto – The work at WOINCOURT for A.H.T. completed.	
"	4th		Sunday – medical inspection of personnel.	
"	5th		Motor lorry sent to Supply Col. workshop for overhaul & repairs. Foden disinfected hospital blankets for 141st C.F. Ambulance: also clothing of 141st C.F.A. + San. Section. Snow fell, about 5 inches.	
"	6th		Parties clearing snow – Foden immobilised on account of snow.	
"	7th + 8th		Snow clearing continued. Foden worked at BOUVAINCOURT for Fort Garry Horse, Canadian Cav. Brig. H.Q.; and X Battery (for A.D.V.S.)	
"	8th Feb.		1 Br. N.C.O. and six sweepers detached for duty with Secunderabad Pioneer Battalion.	
"	9th "		Drill, + smoke helmet practice. Foden (at BOUVAINCOURT) X Battery for A.D.V.S.	
"	10th		route march.	
"	11th		Sunday – medical inspection.	
"	12th		Foden = Lord Strathcona's Horse.	
"	13th		work in camp – drill.	
"	14th		fatigue party Div. H.Q. (coal etc)	
"	15th		fatigue party at DARGNIES (for S.O.D.T.)	

O.C. of N° 5 (Cav.) Sanitary Section

WAR DIARY or INTELLIGENCE SUMMARY.

Army Form C. 2118.

No 5 (Cav.) Sanitary Section

Place	Date	Hour	Summary of Events and Information	Remarks and references to Appendices
BOUVAIN-COURT	16th Feb 1917		Foden at LONGROY, 18th Lancers, disinfected condemned clothing for D.A.P.O.S.	
"	17/2/17		Route march.	
"	18/2/17		Sunday - medical inspection.	
"	19/2/17		Motor Lorry returned after overhaul at Supply Col. workshop. "Thaw Scheme" came into force - Lorry & Foden immobilised.	
"	20th + 21st		Clearing roads at BOUVAINCOURT.	
"	22nd		Fatigue party worked for farmer.	
"	23rd + 24th		Fatigue party worked under R.E. repairing roads. Foden at BOUVAINCOURT disinfected worn out clothing for D.A.D.O.S.	
"	25th		Sunday - Medical Inspection.	
"	26th to 28th Feb 1917		Road repairing under R.E. continued. Party cleaned up billets etc. of signals at DARGNIES.	

R.H. Lee
Capt. I.M.S.
O.C. No 5 (Cav.) Sanitary Section

Feb. 1917

Sanitary Section, 5th Cav. Div.

COMMITTEE FOR THE
MEDICAL HISTORY OF THE WAR
Date 21 MAY 1917

Medical

Sanitary Section,
5th Cavalry Division.

from 1st to 28th February 1917.

Serial No. 291.

WAR DIARY or INTELLIGENCE SUMMARY

No 5 (Cav.) Sanitary Section

Army Form C. 2118.

Place	Date	Hour	Summary of Events and Information	Remarks and references to Appendices
BOUVAINCOURT	1st Feb. 1917		Party at WOINCOURT making horse lines for Auxiliary Horse Transport 5.2	
"	2nd & 3rd		Ditto — the work at WOINCOURT for A.H.T. completed.	
"	4th		Sunday — medical inspection of personnel.	
"	5th		Motor lorry sent to Supply Col. workshop for overhaul & repairs. Foden disinfected hospital blankets for 141st C.F. Ambulance; also clothing of 141st C.F.A. & San. Section. Snow fell, about 5 inches.	
"	6th		Parties clearing snow. Foden immobilised on account of snow.	
"	7th & 8th		Snow clearing continued. Foden worked at BOUVAINCOURT for Fort Garry Horse, Canadian Cav. Brig. H.Q.; and X Battery (for A.D.V.S.)	
"	8th Feb.		1 Br. N.C.O. and six sweepers detached for duty with Secunderabad Pioneer Battalion.	
"	9th "		Drill, & smoke helmet practice. Foden (at BOUVAINCOURT) X Battery for A.D.V.S.	
"	10th "		route march.	
"	11th "		Sunday. medical inspection.	
"	12th "		Foden = Lord Strathcona's Horse.	
"	13th "		work in camp — drill.	
"	14th "		fatigue party Div. H.Q. (coal etc)	
"	15th "		fatigue party at DARGNIES (for S.O.P.T.)	

R. H. Ferguson
O.C. No 5 (Cav) Sanitary Section

WAR DIARY

Army Form C. 2118.

Instructions regarding War Diaries and Intelligence Summaries are contained in F. S. Regs., Part II. and the Staff Manual respectively. Title pages will be prepared in manuscript.

No 5 (Cav.) INTELLIGENCE SUMMARY. (Erase heading not required.) Sanitary Section

Place	Date	Hour	Summary of Events and Information	Remarks and references to Appendices
BOUVAIN-COURT	16th Feb 1917		Foden at LONGROY, 18th Lancers, disinfected condemned clothing for D.A.D.O.S.	
"	17/2/17		route march.	
"	18/2/17		Sunday – medical inspection.	
"	19/2/17		Motor Lorry returned after overhaul at Supply Col workshop. "Thaw Scheme" came into force – Lorry + Foden immobilised.	
"	20th + 21st		Clearing roads at BOUVAINCOURT.	
"	22nd		Fatigue party worked for farmer.	
"	23rd + 24th		Fatigue party worked under R.E. repairing roads. Foden at BOUVAINCOURT disinfected worn out clothing for D.A.D.O.S.	
"	25th		Sunday – Medical Inspection.	
"	26th to 28th Feb 1917		road repairing under R.E. continued. Party cleaned up billets etc. of Signals at DARGNIES.	

R H Lee
Capt. M.S.
O.C. No 5 (Cav) Sanitary Section

April 1917.

Sanitary Section — 5th Cav Div

COMMITTEE FOR THE
MEDICAL HISTORY OF THE WAR
Date -6 JUL. 1917

WAR DIARY or INTELLIGENCE SUMMARY

Army Form C. 2118.

Vol 23

No 5 (Cav.) Sanitary Section

Place	Date	Hour	Summary of Events and Information	Remarks and references to Appendices
VILLERS-BRETONNEUX	1st April 1917		Section moved to VILLERS-BRETONNEUX. Routine work in the billets of Cav. H.Q.	
"	2/4/17		1 N.C.O. and 5 men detached 20th Deccan Horse at FRAMERVILLE. Party at WARFUSEE worked under S.M.O. Ambala Brigade	
"	3/4/17		as on 2nd inst. Foden disinfector to CAPPY for 5th Cav. Reserve Park	
"	4/4/17		Work parties as before. Foden moved to WARFUSEE for Ambala Brigade	
"	5/4/17		Party with Deccan Horse rejoined	
"	6th		1 N.C.O. + 20 men detached at CAPPY, for work under S.M.O. Canadian Cav. Brigade. Foden rejoined	
"	7th		carting manure etc. at Div. H.Q. and routine sanitary work	
"	8th		as on 7th. Foden detached at Poona Horse	
"	9th		ditto. Box respirators fitted & tested in gas chamber by Div. Gas Officer	
"	10th to 13th		Routine work in VILLERS-BRETONNEUX. Foden worked for San. Section	
GUIZANCOURT	14/4/17		Section moved to GUIZANCOURT. 1 N.C.O. + 20 men rejoined from CAPPY. Foden disinfector temp. attached to Div. Supply. Col. at PROYART	
"	15 and 16th		GUIZANCOURT cleaned up, old latrines filled, incinerator built etc.	
"	17th		GUIZANCT. continued. Party at DEVISE for Canad. M.O.S.	
"	18th		Foden (at HERLY with Supp. Col.) commenced work on underclothing of the Div.	
"	19th		Div. H.Q. continued. 1 N.C.O. + 20 men temp. detached at HERLY for Supply Column	
"	20th + 21st		Work at GUIZANCT continued	

R.H. Lee Capt. A.M.S.

WAR DIARY or INTELLIGENCE SUMMARY

Army Form C. 2118.

N° 5 (Cav.) Sanitary Section

Place	Date	Hour	Summary of Events and Information	Remarks and references to Appendices
GUIZANCOURT	22nd April 1917		Work at GUIZANCOURT continued. Detachment rejoined from HERLY.	
"	23rd		1 N.C.O. and 10 men detached at CAULAINCOURT for work under S.M.O. Ambala Brigade. Party worked at TREFCON village and Sec. Brig. H.Q.	
"	24th		Work at GUIZANCOURT — fly-proof latrines + urinals built etc.	
"	25th		Detachment returned from CAULAINCOURT. Party worked at Field Squadron camp near TERTRY.	
"	26 + 27th		Party at TREFCON, built incinerator, dug deep latrine pits etc.	
"	28th + 29th		Party at CAULAINCOURT, cleaning up vicinity of spring + Ambala Brig. baths.	
"	30th		Party cleaning up vicinity of lines of Lord Strathcona's Horse, N. of DEVISE. Party cleaning up billets etc. of Lord ?? Col. at FALVY. commenced pit for deep latrine. Work in GUIZANCOURT continued.	

P.H.Lee
Cpt / M.S.
O.C. N° 5 (Cav.) Sanitary Section

Ypres
1914.

No. 5 (Cav.) (Gas Sect.)

COMMITTEE FOR THE
4 NOV 1919
MEDICAL HISTORY OF THE WAR

D.M.S.
India

Forward copies Brig. T.
Sanitary returns 5th Cav Bde
for week ending 30.4.19.
Please acknowledge.

R McKee
Capt. IMS
O.C. Sanitary Section

5TH
CAVALRY DIVISIONAL
SANITARY SECTION.
No. S/14
Date 7-5-19

WAR DIARY
or
INTELLIGENCE SUMMARY.

Nº 5 (Cav.) Sanitary Section

Army Form C. 2118.

Place	Date	Hour	Summary of Events and Information	Remarks and references to Appendices
VILLERS-BRETONNEUX	1st April 1917		Section moved to VILLERS-BRETONNEUX. Routine works in the billets of Div. H.Q.	
"	2/4/17		1 N.C.O. and 15 men detached 20th Deccan Horse at FRAMERVILLE. Party at WARFUSEE worked under S.M.O. Ambala Brigade.	
"	3/4/17		as on 2nd inst. Foden disinfector to CAPPY for 5th Cav. Reserve Park.	
"	4/4/17		Work parties as before. Foden moved to WARFUSEE for Ambala Brigade.	
"	5/4/17		Party with Deccan Horse rejoined.	
"	6—		1 N.C.O. + 20 men detached at CAPPY, for work under S.M.O. Canadian Cav. Brigade. Foden rejoined.	
"	7th		carting manure etc. at Div. H.Q. and routine sanitary work.	
"	8th		as on 7th. Foden detached at Poona Horse.	
"	9—		ditto. Box respirators fitted & tested in gas chamber by Divl. Gas Officer.	
"	10th to 13th		Routine work in VILLERS-BRETONNEUX. Foden worked for San. Section.	
GUIZANCOURT	14/4/17		Section moved to GUIZANCOURT. 1 N.C.O. + 20 men rejoined from CAPPY. Foden disinfector temp. attached to Divl. Supply Col. at PROYART.	
"	15th and 16th		GUIZANCOURT cleaned up, old latrines filled, incinerator built etc.	
"	17th		GUIZANCT. continued. Party at DEVISE for Canad. M.G.S.	
"	18th		Foden (at HERLY with Supp. Col.) commences work on underclothing of the Divn.	
"	19th		Div. H.Q. continued. 1 N.C.O. + 20 men temp. detached at HERLY, for Supply Column	
"	20th + 21st		work at GUIZANCT. continued.	

R.H. Lee Capt. I.M.S.

WAR DIARY
or
INTELLIGENCE SUMMARY.

(Erase heading not required.)

Army Form C. 2118.

Instructions regarding War Diaries and Intelligence Summaries are contained in F. S. Regs., Part II. and the Staff Manual respectively. Title pages will be prepared in manuscript.

No 5 (Cav.) Sanitary Section

Place	Date	Hour	Summary of Events and Information	Remarks and references to Appendices
GUIZANCOURT	22nd April 1917		Work at GUIZANCOURT continued. Detachment rejoined from HERLY.	
"	23rd		1 N.C.O. and 10 men detached at CAULAINCOURT for work under S.M.O. Ambala Brigade. Party worked at TREFCON village and Sec. Brig. H.Q.	
"	24th		Work at GUIZANCOURT — fly-proof latrines + urinals built etc.	
"	25th		Detachment returned from CAULAINCOURT. Party worked at Field Squadron camp near TERTRY.	
"	26 + 27th		Party at TREFCON, built incinerator, dug deep latrine pits etc.	
"	28th + 29th		Party at CAULAINCOURT, cleaning up vicinity of spring + Ambala Brig. baths.	
"	30th		Party cleaning up vicinity of lines of Lord Strathcona's Horse, N. of DEVISE. Party cleaning up billets etc. of Div. Amn. Col. at FALVY. Commenced pit for deep latrine. Work in GUIZANCOURT continued.	

R.F. Lee
Capt. I.M.S.
O.C. No 5 (Cav.) Sanitary Section

Mar. 1917.

Sanitary Section — 5th Cav. Div.

COMMITTEE FOR THE
MEDICAL HISTORY OF THE WAR
Date -6 JUL. 1917

WAR DIARY or INTELLIGENCE SUMMARY.

Vol XXII.

Army Form C. 2118.

No 5 (Cav.) Sanitary Section

Place	Date	Hour	Summary of Events and Information	Remarks and references to Appendices
BOUVAIN-COURT.	1st March 1917.		Party mending roads, under R.E. Foden Disinfector worked for Sec'bad M.G. Squad. + Mhow I.C.F.A.	
"	2/3/31		Party on roads (R.E.). Foden = Sec'bad I.C.F.A.	
"	3rd		ditto	
"	4th		Sunday - medical inspection of unit.	
"	5th		Party on roads (R.E.) Foden = X Battery at INCHEVILLE.	
"	6th		Party on roads (R.E.)	
"	7th		ditto. Foden at DARGNIES, working for D.A.D.O.S. (cast clothing)	
"	8th + 9th		Party on roads (R.E).	
"	10th		Party at WOINCOURT, cleaned drains. Foden = Supply Col. at MERS.	
"	11th		WOINCOURT continued. Party on roads, (R.E.)	
"	12th + 13th		Parties on road mending under R.E.	
"	14th		Foden at St QUENTIN for R.C.H.A. Brigade. 1 N.C.O. + 6 men returned from Sec'bad Pioneer Batt'n	
"	15th		Party on roads (R.E.) Foden worked for Lord Strathconas Horse	
"	16th		ditto. Foden = 9th Hodson's Horse at MONTIERES.	
"	17th		ditto. Foden = Canadian Cav. Brig. at TULLY	
"	18th		Sunday, medical inspection.	
"	19th		Foden at AIGNEVILLE, for Sec'bad Cav. Brig.	

R.H. Lee
Capt. A.M.S.
O.C. No 5 (Cav.) Sanitary Section

WAR DIARY
or
INTELLIGENCE SUMMARY

Army Form C. 2118.

No 5 (Cav.) Sanitary Section

(Erase heading not required.)

Instructions regarding War Diaries and Intelligence Summaries are contained in F. S. Regs., Part II. and the Staff Manual respectively. Title pages will be prepared in manuscript.

Place	Date	Hour	Summary of Events and Information	Remarks and references to Appendices
BOUVAIN- COURT	20th March 1917		Men detached rejoined unit as under :— 7 men from R.S.O. at WOINCOURT — 3 men from Div. H.Q. 2 men from Div. School at AULT. Parties cleaned up DARGNIES and BOUVAINCOURT. 1 N.C.O. and 20 men with kit etc. moved to SENARPONT.	
REVELLES	21/3/17		Whole Section moved to billets in REVELLES.	
CACHY	22/3/17		Section moved to CACHY, less Foden disinfector which broke down in AMIENS.	
"	23/3/17		Advised O.C. Workshop Supp. Col. re Foden — Small box respirators fitted. Under ½ hr. notice to move from 10 A.M.	
near HERBE- COURT	24/3/17		½ the section moved to 1 mile S. of HERBECOURT, on H.—ASSEVILLERS road; road here impassable for lorry, which returned to CACHY.	
HERBECT.	25/3/17		Moved to HERBECOURT where lorry with rest of Section joined in afternoon. 1 N.C.O. and 6 men detached at PERONNE, Div. H.Q., under D.A.D.M.S.	
"	26/3/17		1 N.C.O. + 20 men detached at PERONNE (making total 2 N.C.O.s + 26 men). 4 men detached to 141st Sec bad I.C.F.A. at BOIS DE MEREAUCOURT. 1 man detached to 3rd Corps Dressing Station at PROYART. Party worked at Sec bad Brig. dug-outs + bivouacs in BOIS de MEREAUCT.	
"	27/3/17		Work in BOIS DE MEREAUCOURT continued.	

R.F.R. Lee Capt. A.M.S.
O.C. No 5 (Cav.) Sanitary Section

WAR DIARY or INTELLIGENCE SUMMARY.

No 5 (Cav.) Sanitary Section

Army Form C. 2118.

Place	Date	Hour	Summary of Events and Information	Remarks and references to Appendices
HERBECOURT	28th March 1917		Party continued work in BOIS DE MEREAUCOURT. 1 N.C.O. + 1 sweeper detached at B Echelon camp near BIACHES, of which I have been put in additional medical charge. Foden, having been repaired, rejoined the Section. It is now without coal which cannot be obtained.	
CAMP No East of CAPPY	29/3/17		Section (less 1 N.C.O. and 12 men at Div. H.Q. at PERONNE) moved to camp No 56 B.1 mile East of CAPPY, and joined B Echelon of the 5th Cav. Divn. Foden moved with wood fuel. General Sanitary work in camp: dug latrine for Indians, etc.	
ditto	30/3/17		1 N.C.O. + 12 men rejoined from Div. H.Q. at PERONNE. Work in camp continued, buried horses etc.	
	31/3/17		Work in camp continued: buried more horses. 1000 lb. coal obtained from 48th Division Coal Dump on urgent indent. B Echelon troops rejoined their units.	

R.H. Lee
Capt. I.M.S.
O.C. No 5 (Cav.) Sanitary Section

"Medical".

Serial No. 294.

Sanitary Section, 5th Cavalry Division.

From 1st May to 30th June 1917.

May & June 1917

Sanitary Section — 5th Cav. Div.

COMMITTEE FOR THE
MEDICAL HISTORY OF THE WAR
Date 27 JUL. 1917

WAR DIARY
or
INTELLIGENCE SUMMARY

No 5 (Cav.) Sanitary Section

Army Form C. 2118.

VOL. XXIV

Place	Date	Summary of Events and Information	Remarks and references to Appendices
GUIZANCOURT	1/5/17	10 sweepers under a Jemadar Sweeper detached to 104th Labour I.C.F.A. for work in Ambala Brigade area. Work at FALVY completed.	
"	2/5/17	Parties at camp L.S. Horse near DEVISE and N Batty at MONCHY-LAGACHE, general scavenging, burning rubbish, filling old latrines, making rough incinerators, manure dumps, sullage pits.	
"	3rd	Inspected water supply available for Divn. Reinforcement in HOLNON WOOD & reported to A.D.M.S.	
"	4th and 5th	Took over duties of D.A.D.M.S. temp. of 5th Cav. Div. temp. Party at 7th D.O. camp; made manure incinerators etc.	
"	6th	Sunday - usual routine:- medical inspection, drill, s.b. respirator practice, washing clothes and bathes.	
"	7th	Party to Aux. H. Transport at EPANANCOURT. Their water-cart condemned; in bad repair.	
"	8th	2 men sent to work in workshop of 81st San. Section for instruction.	
"	9th	Party cleaned up area evacuated by R.C.H.A. Brigade near FOURQUES. Their Amm. Col. camp dirty:- reported to A.D.M.S.	
"	10th	Party to Can. M.G.S. near DEVISE, erecting latrines etc. Inspected Ambala Brigade baths at CAULAINCOURT - six sprays, in good order:- Sullage pits + baffle plates.	
"	11th	Can. M.G.S. continued - army whole unit due for reinoc. T.A.B. 10 men given 1st dose.	
"	12th	Can. M.G.S. finished.	
"	13th	Sunday routine.	
"	14th	Adv. party to NOBESCOURT FARM - Interviewed O.C. 59th San. Section. 6 sweepers detached for duty with Sec. Sec. dismounted Brigade.	

R.H. Lee Capt I.M.S.
O.C. No 5 (Cav.) San. Section

WAR DIARY or INTELLIGENCE SUMMARY

Army Form C. 2118.

No. 5 (Cav.) Sanitary Section

Place	Date	Hour	Summary of Events and Information	Remarks and references to Appendices
GUIZANCOURT	14th May 1917		During the time the unit were at GUIZANCOURT this place was provided with permanent fly-proof latrines, urinals, sullage pits & grease traps, incinerator, manure dumps etc; rubbish burnt & numerous old latrines filled in.	
Camp at Q.1.b.3.9. (62c 40,000)	15th		The unit moved to bivouac at Q.1.b.3.9. the work of making latrines urinals etc etc. for Div. H.Q. at NOBESCOURT FARM commenced.	
"	16th			
"	17th		4 men temp. detached to 141st Sec bad I.C.F.A. and 4 men temp. detached to Sec bad Divn. Brigade	
"	18th		Party of 11 men returned from 104th Inhow I.C.F.A. — attended a conference of O.C. 59th & 61st San. Sections + D.A.D.M.S. Cav. Corps + D.A.D.M.S. 5th Cav. Div. With O.C. 59th San. Sect. visited Brigade Baths at MONTIGNY FARM, and JEANCOURT, A.D.S., and wells being sunk in village.	
"	20th		Attended a conference at Cav. Corps H.Q. of D.D.M.S. Cav. Corps, San. Officer 4th Army, all D.A.D.M.S. of Cav. Divisions and O.C. Sanitary Sections. Areas for latter allotted except to 4th and 5th (Cav.) Sanitary Sections, both Indian units, which owing to their constitution (4 British ranks) are not capable of taking charge of an area. They are to work in the areas, and under the supervision of the 59th and 61st Sanitary Sections. The San. Officer 4th Army lectured on the duties of San. Sections generally; — best method of dealing with manure is burning, but whether in small heaps or in incinerators not agreed on — Pointed out that Cav. regts with half their men in trenches will not be able to burn all manure — In wet weather, close packing. All methods require constant care and some skill. It was pointed out that units concerned, and not the San. Sect., were responsible for sanitation.	

R.H. Rye Capt. RAMC
O.S. No 5 (Cav.) San. Section

WAR DIARY or INTELLIGENCE SUMMARY

No. 5 (Cav.) Sanitary Section

Army Form C. 2118.

Place	Date	Summary of Events and Information	Remarks and references to Appendices
Camp at Q.1.6 & 8.1 (62c 1/40,000)	22/5/17	Inspected A.D.S. of 7th Can. F.A. at VADENCOURT; also Can. Div. Brig. H.Q. at VADENCOURT chateau, + examined water of spring in grotto: report to A.D.M.S.	
"	23rd	Inspected PONTRU and trenches held by Can. Div. Brig. and reported to A.D.M.S.:- (water supply good spring in PONTRU — no fly-proof latrines)	
K.32.b.4.1 (62c 1/40,000)	24th	Moved camp to K.32.b.4.1 (62c 1/40,000)	
"	25th	Party cleaned up billets and burnt rubbish at MONTECOURT. Inspected Ambala Br. H.Q. 8th Hussars, 9th Hodson's H., 18th Lancers and X Battery (all "back-area" details) and reported to A.D.M.S.	
"	26th	Party to Adv. H.T.G. 27 near TERTRY:- dug some latrines + sullage pits: started manure-burning + all heaps near horse lines netted.	
"	29th	Section given special work of preparing Adrian Huts etc. at the Sucrerie BERNES for a M.D.S.; making latrines, digging pits, bricking floors, removing bunks etc: all available men of section + 12 Kahars of Lucknow I.C. F.A.	
"	30th	BERNES cont.; 1 Jemadar + 4 sweepers attached temp. to 104th Mhow I.C. F.A.	
"	31st	BERNES continued.	

R.F.H. [signature]
Capt. I.M.S.
O.C. No. 5 (Cav.) Sanitary Section

WAR DIARY or INTELLIGENCE SUMMARY

Army Form C. 2118.

No. 5 (Cav.) Sanitary Section

Place	Date	Summary of Events and Information	Remarks and references to Appendices
Camp near NOBESCOURT FARM (Map 62c K.32 b 4.1)	1st June 1917	Work at BERNES (Sucrerie) for new M.D.S. continued.	
"	2/6/17	ditto	
"	3/6/17	Sunday routine – No. 7032 2/Cpl. R.H. LOVERIDGE R.A.M.C. was detached to Artists Rifles with a view to receiving a permanent commission.	
"	4th	BERNES cont. – work at Div. H.Q. Inspected + reported on Divs. H.T. and Supp. Col.	
"	5th	BERNES cont. – 5 sweepers returned from 104th F.C.F.A. Inspected + reported on back area of the three Canadian Cav. Regt.	
"	6th to 7th	BERNES cont. – and Div. H.Q. improved by making manure incinerators, urinals, ablution benches etc.	
"	8th	Inspected 5th Cav. Res. Park, N Batty and X Batt. R.H.A. 16th Lancers, Amm. Col. 17th Brig. R.H.A. and R.C.H.A Bdg. Amm. Col. with especial reference to water carts	
"	9th	Interviewed A.C. VERMAND and arranged work party. Insp. w. carts of 10th Lancers + 8th Hussars. Report to A.D.M.S. on water supply of VERMAND advising closing of Water Point in R 26 b (62c) east for horses, and opening of a W.P. at a spring at R.32 c 7.9.	
"	11th	Work party 1 N.C.O. + 10 sweepers at VERMAND. Inspected Canad. M.G.S, 14th M.G.S.	
"	12th	VERMAND cont. – Inspected 13th M.G.S. – Interviewed A.C. TREFCON + arranged work party. Lecture to water-duty details at CAULAINCOURT.	
"	13th	Work party at CAULAINCOURT. Inspected Div. Amm. Park – Lecture on water duties at DEVISE	
"	14th	5 sweepers returned from 141st F.C.F.A. 2 sweepers detached to party Ind. Detaching Cav. entrenching Bn at VERMAND. Inspected A + B Batteries R.C.H.A. wagon lines, and D 29.B. R.F.A. Reported to A.D.M.S. on result of inspections of water carts of units in div. area.	

R.H.L. Capt. I/M.S.
O.C. No 5 (Cav) Sanitary Section.

WAR DIARY or INTELLIGENCE SUMMARY

Army Form C. 2118.

No 5 (Cav.) Sanitary Section

Place	Date	Summary of Events and Information	Remarks and references to Appendices
Camp near NOBESCOURT FARM (1/62d K 32 b 4,1)	15th June 1917	Attended conference of O.C. Sanitary Sections of Cav. Corps under D.A.D.M.S. Cav. Corps. Inspected work at TREFCON (chiefly scavenging) 7th Dr. Guards and Ambala Brig. Baths. 2 sweepers, detached to Secunderabad Cavm. Brig. on 12/5/17, rejoined the section.	
"	16th	TREFCON finished, including work for Secunderabad M.V.S., also two incinerators for 13th M.G.S. Interviewed Water Officer Cav. Corps re water supply VERMAND. Suggestions detailed above (v. 9th inst.) to be adopted.	
"	17th	Work party at VENDELLES, cleaning up, filling old latrines, making incinerators, sullage pits etc. for Ind. Cav. Mounted Reinforcements & other details.	
"	18th	Visited School of Sanitation at PERONNE — Inspected work at VENDELLES (cont.) 2 latrines completed.	
"	19th	Party at TERTRY doing scavenging. Inspected new lines of 5th Cav. Reserve Park; also the ration dumps of the three Brigades of 5th Cav. Divn, and defects pointed out to respective B.S.O's	
"	20th	TERTRY cont. — Party at VENDELLES digging pits for Indian latrines (2) and same completed. Attended weekly conference of O.C. S.S. at Corps H.Q.	
"	21st to 23rd	Party at MONCHY-LAGACHE — Cloud incinerator built, fire type latrines made fly-proof, 55 old latrines filled in, and a large quantity of rubbish burnt —	
"	24th	Inspected VENDELLES and reported to A.D.M.S. that baths near R 14 a 2,2 were too near well the only good source of water in the village, & recommended their removal & treatment of sullage pit with lime.	
"	25th	Interview with A.D.C. MONTECOURT. Report to A.D.M.S. that Water Point at MONTECOURT near V 11 d. 6,9 should be closed except for horses, as the source is R. OMIGNON, and there is good W.P. at V 4 c. 6,2 — Party working at Divl. H.Q. 1 Officer's latrine erected — Manure packed & treated with C. solution.	

R.H. Lee Capt. A.M.S.
O.C. No 5 (Cav.) Sanitary Section

WAR DIARY or INTELLIGENCE SUMMARY.

No 5 (Cav) Sanitary Section

Army Form C. 2118.

Place	Date	Hour	Summary of Events and Information	Remarks and references to Appendices
Camp near NOBESCOURT FARM (Map 62c) K 32 b 4.1	24th June 1917		Sunday routine for personnel — Examined well in VENDELLES near R 1 d 1.5 water muddy and requires more than 2 measures of chloride of lime per 100 gal. It is much inferior to well at R 1 d 2.2. Verbal report to A.D.M.S. as above and confirming my report and recommendations of 21st inst. (v. supra)	
"	25th		MONCHY-LAGACHE continued — 4 sweepers temp. detached to Ambala Brig. Dismounted Reinforcements at VENDELLES. Party at VENDELLES moving site of Br. latrine. Interview with A.C. of	
"	26th		VRAIGNES and work party arranged. Party at VRAIGNES, scavenging, filling old latrines etc.	
"	27th		VRAIGNES cont. — Party at LE VERGUIER oiling ponds and filling old latrines — Party at BOUVINCT cleaning up chateau for G.O.C's quarters. Conference of San. Sections at Cav. Corps H.Q.	
"	28th		BOUVINCOURT continued.	
"	29th		LE VERGUIER completed — BOUVINCOURT cont. latrine trench dug — Inspected 5th Cav. Div. Recce Party, Canadian M.V.S. and Ambala Sec'd and Canadian Ration Dumps. defects noted on 19th inst. had not been remedied in the Ambala Br. ration dump: report to A.D.M.S. accordingly; also drawing attention to Corps R.O. No 221 of 20/5/17 — Imp. Fort Garry Horse.	
"	30th		BOUVINCOURT continued. Latrine made & completed for new camp of D.A.D.O.S. Cav. Div.	

R.H. Lee
Capt. T.M.S.
O.C. No 5 (Cav.) Sanitary Section

May
1919

No. 5 (Lov.) San. Sect.

COMMITTEE FOR THE
4 NOV 1919
MEDICAL HISTORY OF THE WAR

WAR DIARY or **INTELLIGENCE SUMMARY.**

Army Form C. 2118.

No 5 (Cav.) Sanitary Section.

Place	Date	Hour	Summary of Events and Information	Remarks and references to Appendices
GUIZANCOURT	1/5/17		10 sweepers under a Jemadar Sweeper detached to 104th Indian I.C.F.A. for work in Ambala Brigade area. Work at FALVY completed.	
"	2/5/17		Parties at camp L.S. Horse near DEVISE and N Battery at MONCHY-LAGACHE, general scavenging, burning rubbish, filling old latrines, making rough incinerators, manure dumps, sullage pits etc.	
"	3rd		Inspected water supply available for Divn. Reinforcement in HOLNON WOOD & reported to A.D.M.S.	
"	4th and 5th		Took over duties of D.A.D.M.S. temp. of 5th Cav. Div. temp. Party at 7th D.G. camp; made manure incinerators etc.	
"	6th		Sunday – usual routine :– medical inspection, drill, s.b. respirator practice, washing clothes and bathes.	
"	7th		Party to Aux. H. Transport at EPANANCOURT. Their water-cart condemned; in bad repair.	
"	8th		2 men sent to work in workshop of 61st San. Section for instruction.	
"	9th		Party cleaned up area evacuated by R.C.H.A. Brigade near FOURQUES. Their camp dirty :– reported to A.D.M.S.	
"	10th		Party to Can. M.G.S. near DEVISE, erecting latrines etc. Inspected Ambala Brigade bathes at CAULAINCOURT – six sprays, in good order. Sullage pits & baffle-plates.	
"	11th		Can. M.G.S. continued – nearly whole unit due for reinoc. T.A.B. 18 men given 1st dose.	
"	12th		Can. M.G.S. finished.	
"	13th		Sunday routine.	
"	14th		Adv. party to NOBESCOURT FARM – Interviewed O.C. 59th San. Section. 6 sweepers detached for duty with Sec bad dismounted Brigade.	

R H Lee Capt. I.M.S.
O.C. No 5 (Cav.) San. Section

WAR DIARY
or
INTELLIGENCE SUMMARY.

Army Form C. 2118.

No. 5 (Cav.) Sanitary Section

Place	Date	Hour	Summary of Events and Information	Remarks and references to Appendices
GUIZANCOURT	14th May 1917		During the time the unit were at GUIZANCOURT this place was provided with permanent fly-proof latrines, urinals, sullage pits + grease traps, incinerator, manure dumps etc: rubbish burnt + numerous old latrines filled in.	
Camp at Q.1.b.8.9. (62c 1/40,000)	15th		The unit moved to bivouac at Q.1.b.8.9. The work of making latrines urinals etc etc. for Div. H.Q. at NOBESCOURT FARM commenced.	
"	16th			
"	17th		4 men temp. detached to 141st Sec'bad I.C.F.A. and 4 men temp. detached to Sec'bad Dism. Brigade	
"	18th		Party of 11 men returned from 104th Mhow I.C.F.A. — attended a conference of O.C. 59th + 61st San. Sections + D.A.D.M.S. Cav. Corps + D.A.D.M.S. 5th Cav. Div. With O.C. 59th San. Sect. visited Brigade Baths at MONTIGNY FARM, and JEANCOURT, A.D.S., and wells being sunk in village.	
"	20th		Attended a conference at Cav. Corps H.Q. of D.D.M.S. Cav. Corps, San. Officer 4th Army, all D.A.D.M.S. of Cav. Divisions and O.C. Sanitary Sections. Areas for latter allotted except to 4th and 5th (Cav.) Sanitary Sections, both Indian units, which owing to their constitution (4 British ranks), are not capable of taking charge of an area. They are to work in the areas, and under the supervision of the 59th and 61st Sanitary Sections. The San. Officer 4th Army lectured on the duties of San. Sections generally:— best method of dealing with manure is burning, but whether in small heaps or in incinerators not agreed on. Pointed out that Cav. regts with half their men in trenches will not be able to burn all manure. In wet weather close packing. All methods require constant care and some skill. It was pointed out that units concerned, and not the San. Sect., were responsible for sanitation.	

R.H. Lee Capt. R.A.M.S.
O.C. No 5 (Cav.) San. Section

WAR DIARY or INTELLIGENCE SUMMARY.

Army Form C. 2118.

N° 5 (Cav.) Sanitary Section

Place	Date	Hour	Summary of Events and Information	Remarks and references to Appendices
camp at Q.1.b.8.9 (62c 1/40,000)	22/5/17		Inspected A.D.S. of 7th Can. F.A. at VADENCOURT; also Can. Cav. Brig. H.Q. at VADENCOURT chateau, + examined water of spring in grotto: report to A.D.M.S.	
"	23rd		Inspected PONTRU and trenches held by Can. Cav. Brig. and reported to A.D.M.S.:- (water supply good spring in PONTRU — no fly-proof latrines)	
K.32.b.4.1 (62c 1/40,000)	24th		moved camp to K.32.b.4.1 (62c 1/40,000)	
"	25th		Party cleaned up billets and burnt rubbish at MONTECOURT. Inspected Ambala Br. H.Q. 8th Hussars, 9th Hodson's H. 18th Lancers and X Battery (all "back-area" details) and reported to A.D.M.S.	
"	28th		Party to Aux. H.T. Coy near TERTRY — dug some latrines + sullage pits: started manure-burning small heaps near horse lines method.	
"	29th		Section given special work of preparing Adrian Huts etc. at the Sucrerie BERNES for a M.D.S.; making latrines, digging pits, bricking floors, removing bunks etc; all available men of section + 12 Kahars of Lucknow 1.C.F.A.	
"	30th		BERNES cont.; 1 Jemadar + 4 sweepers detached temp. to 104th Mhow I.C.F.A.	
"	31st		BERNES continued —	

R.H.S. Capt. I.M.S.
O.C. N° 5 (Cav.) Sanitary Section

COMMITTEE FOR THE
MEDICAL HISTORY OF THE WAR
Date 16 OCT 1917

"Medical." Serial No: 294.

5th Cavalry Sanitary Section.

From 1st to 31st July 1917.

WAR DIARY or ~~INTELLIGENCE SUMMARY.~~ N° 5 (Cav.) Sanitary Section

Army Form C. 2118.

Place	Date	Hour	Summary of Events and Information	Remarks and references to Appendices
Camp near MONTESCOURT FARM K 32 C 4.1 Map 62 c 1:40,000	1st July 1917		Sunday routine for personnel — Inspected Div. Aux. Horse Transport, Reserve Park, X Battery R.H.A., Div. Amm. Column and Canadian Amm. Column especially re manure.	
	2nd		N° 52700 9 A/Serg. H.R. HODGES temp. detached to School of Sanitation PERONNE for a course in constructional work. Parties at BOUVINCOURT and VRAIGNES — Indian latrine completed for rations dump near MONTESCOURT.	
"	3rd		BOUVINCOURT cont. — Party packing manure at Amm. Col. and covering with earth. Inspected Sec'bad Brigade (back area) esp. re manure disposal.	
"	4th		Conference at Cav. Corps H.Q. Parties to Amm. Col. and to MONTIGNY packing + covering manure, filling refuse pits, repairing deep latrines etc.	
"	5th		BOUVINCT. + MONTIGNY continued.	
"	6th		Pumping out + disinfecting old rain water cisterns which had been fouled + were smelling badly at BOUVINCOURT chateau. Interviewed A.C. of VERMAND and inspecting new drinking Water Point N° 7. Inspected A and B Batteries R.C.H.A. horse lines, especially re manure disposal.	
"	7th		Party at BOUVINCOURT digging latrine pits etc.	
"	8th		Sunday routine — Inspected lines evacuated by 8th Hussars, 14th M.G.S., Ambala Brig. H.Q. near CAULAINCOURT.	

R.H. Lee Capt. R.A.M.S.
O.C. N° 5 (Cav.) Sanitary Section

WAR DIARY or INTELLIGENCE SUMMARY

Army Form C. 2118.

No 5 (Cav.) Sanitary Section

Place	Date	Hour	Summary of Events and Information	Remarks and references to Appendices
Camp near NOBESCOURT FARM (Sh. 62c 1/40,000 K 32 b 4.1)	9th July 1917		Advanced party moved to BOUVINCOURT, where work on latrines etc. continued.	
BOUVINCOURT	10th July		Section moved to BOUVINCOURT with Div. H.Q. Party cleaned up NOBESCOURT area.	
"	11th		Work at BOUVINCOURT cont. Inspected camps of the F.G.H., L.S.H., and R.C.D. with O.C. 59th (area) Sanitary Section, especially re manure.	
"	12th		Inspected regts of Secunderabad Brig. 13th M.G.S. X + N Batteries, 18th Lancers, 9th Hodson's H. and A.H.T. re manure disposal. Work in BOUVINCT. cont.	
"	13th		Party (20 sweepers) to 7th D.G.'s manure dump at TREFCON, concentrating & covering manure. Inspected area evacuated by Res. Park: also lines of Can. M.V.S., M.G.S., and 3 Can. Regts. Billets of A.S.C. at BOUVINCOURT cleaned up after they were evacuated. Manure of all 5th Cav. Div. details collected + burnt.	
"	14th		Foden steam disinfector rejoined. Party cleaned up evacuated lines of X Battery, 14th M.G.S. and 18th Hussars as necessary. Inspected latter also A + B Batts with O.C. 59th S.S.	
"	15th		Party to evac. lines of Cav. Brigade, cleaning up as necessary, covering manure dumps etc.	
ST POL	16th		The Section moved to bivouac at ST POL, near Communal College. Party cleaned up BOUVINCOURT. 10 sweepers daily to scavenge ST POL, help at rubbish dump, empty latrine buckets etc. under the area San. Section No 32. All new messes & billets of 5th Cav. Div. in ST POL inspected.	
"	17th		Party to clean up CHAPELLE ROCOURT	

R.H. Lee Capt. I.M.S.

WAR DIARY
or
INTELLIGENCE SUMMARY.

(Erase heading not required.)

No 5 (Cav.) Sanitary Section

Army Form C. 2118.

Instructions regarding War Diaries and Intelligence Summaries are contained in F. S. Regs., Part II. and the Staff Manual respectively. Title pages will be prepared in manuscript.

Place	Date	Hour	Summary of Events and Information	Remarks and references to Appendices
St POL	18/7/17		Preparing latrines etc. for Div. H.Q. and Div. Troops in ST POL. Interview O.C. 32 San. Section and Town Major ST POL.	
"	19th		Party to ST MICHEL and ROELLECOURT, incinerator built and area of Ambala Brig. cleaned up which had been left in a dirty condition by Australian troops. Deep flyproof latrines constructed for Supply Col. etc and their billets inspected.	
"	20th		Party to ROELLECOURT - further cleaning: repairs to latrines, urinals constructed etc, for Ambala H.Q. and Signals. Inspected CROIX whence F.G. Horse are moving. At ST POL manure dump commenced for Div. H.Q. details. M.M.P. billets in town cleared of manure. Inspected GAUCHIN	
"	21st		Street cleaning and clearing drains etc in ST POL. Provided latrines (pail) for 7th Can. F.A. hospital in ST POL.	
"	22nd		Sunday routine, medical inspection of personnel, respirators etc.	
"	23rd		Foden worked for Div. Troops in ST POL.	
"	24th		Party to ST MICHEL, 8th Hussars area: billets cleaned: old latrines closed: sullage pits dug etc. ST MICHEL continued clearing drains, spraying manure etc. Party to CROIX, Can. Cav. Brig. H.Q.	
"	25th		CROIX cont. fitting latrines etc, Party to ROELLECOURT for 14th M.G.S.	
"	26th		CROIX finished. Party to ROELLECOURT for 18th Lancers. Foden disinfector to MONCHY-CAYEUX for N Battery and 20th Deccan Horse.	

PH Lee Capt. I.MS

WAR DIARY or INTELLIGENCE SUMMARY

Army Form C. 2118

No 5 (Cav.) Sanitary Section

Place	Date	Hour	Summary of Events and Information	Remarks and references to Appendices
St POL	27th July 1917		Party to OSTREVILLE (9th Hodson's Horse). Water supplies of Can. Cav. Brigade tested: excellent sources in all villages. Party street cleaning in St POL. Inspected 9th H.H. and Baths at ROELLECOURT.	
"	28th		Party cleaned up evacuated lines of N Battery at SAUTRECI. and R.C.H.A. Bry. at CHAPPELLE ROCOURT. Horrock's tests of chief sources of water supply of Ambala Brigade: very good results.	
"	29th		Sunday routine – medical inspection of personnel etc.	
"	30th		Party to L'ABBAYE DE NEUVILLE and THIEULOYE, evac. areas of X Battery and Div. Amm. Col.; lines found in very clean condition.	
"	31st		Party to clean up HEUCHIN (new Div. H.Q.). Two sweepers temp. detached at Div. H.Q. for duty. Parties street cleaning and cleaning up evac. lines of Div. H.Q. at St POL.	

R.H.L.
Capt. I.M.S.
O.C. No 5 (Cav.) Sanitary Section

Aug 1917

5th Ind. Cav. Div. San. Sect.

COMMITTEE FOR THE
MEDICAL HISTORY OF THE WAR
Date 16 OCT. 1917

"Medical."

5th Cavalry Sanitary Section.

From 1st to 31st August 1917.

Serial No. 294.

WAR DIARY or INTELLIGENCE SUMMARY

Army Form C. 2118

No 5 (Cav.) Sanitary Section

Place	Date	Hour	Summary of Events and Information	Remarks and references to Appendices
St POL	1st Aug. 1917		Inspected new Div. H.Q. at HEUCHIN - Party erecting latrines etc. Foden lent to Third Army Physical Training School ST POL.	
"	2/8/17		HEUCHIN cont. In consequence of persistent rain, moved from bivouacs to camp in huts on BETHUNE Rd. Foden at Lord Strathcona's Horse -	
"	3rd		heavy rain - work in new camp.	
"	4th		HEUCHIN cont. -	
"	5th		Sunday routine, medical inspection etc.	
"	6th		Party in ST POL, cleaning etc ration dump etc. Inspected A.H.T. and evacuated lines of R.P. at RAMECT. Foden worked for 9th Hodson's Horse and A.H.T.	
"	7th		Party at HEUCHIN - Inspected lines of 7th D.Gs and L.S.H. Foden = 1st D.Gs + Poona H.	
"	8th		Party at RAMECT. cleaned evac. area of R.P. and fitted latrines etc. + tested water supplies of A.H.T. Inspected new lines of R.P. at BRYAS. Foden worked for Fort Garry Horse + R.C. Dragoons.	
"	9th		Party at HEUCHIN - Foden worked for Reserve Park.	
"	10th		HEUCHIN continued -	
"	11th		Party at BRYAS, Reserve Park - latrine pit, sullage pits, incinerator etc made. Interview G.S.O.3 re sanitary arrangements for Horse Show.	

R.H. Lee
Capt. I.M.S.

WAR DIARY
or
INTELLIGENCE SUMMARY

Army Form C. 2118

No 5 (Cav.) Sanitary Section

Place	Date	Hour	Summary of Events and Information	Remarks and references to Appendices
ST POL	12th Aug. 1917		Sunday routine; medical inspection of personnel etc. Foden to 8th Hussars	
"	13/8/17		Party at OSTREVILLE, 9th Horse, repairs to latrines, old trenches filled in etc. Foden to 34th Horse. Inspected billets & lines of 13th M.G.S. at FLEURY. No fly-proof latrines, urinals etc. Foden to 20th H.	
"	14th		Party at BRYAS erecting & screening latrines & urinals for Div. Horse Show.	
"	15th		" ditto " in dismantling same — Billet of suspected scarlatina case at HEUCHIN disinfected; bedding disinfected by Foden. Foden to Can. M.G.S.	
"	16th		Party to FLEURY, 13th M.G.S. fitting latrines, urinals, sullage pits. Water tested (Horrock's) and only good well marked. Interview with S.M.O. Sec'bad Brigade re latrines in lowlying area near river TERNOISE. Foden = 14th M.G.S. and 104th I.C., F.A.	
"	17th		Work at FLEURY completed. Interview with D.A.D.M.S. re alterations required in sanitary arrangements at HEUCHIN. Foden = 5th Field Squadron R.E.	
"	18th		Party to MONCHY-CAYEUX, fitting latrines for Deccan Horse & Poona Horse (at EPS) moved incinerator at HEUCHIN, which was causing a nuisance by smoke.	
"	19th		Sunday routine; party to HEUCHIN, to fit latrine for No 1 Mess. Handed over temp. command of unit to ~~Capt. Matthews~~ Capt. J.A. Macleod R.A.M.C. and proceeded on leave to U.K.	

R.H. Lee Capt. R.A.M.S.
O.C. No 5 (Cav.) Sanitary Section

WAR DIARY
or
INTELLIGENCE SUMMARY

No 5 (Cav) Sanitary Section

Army Form C. 2118

Place	Date	Hour	Summary of Events and Information	Remarks and references to Appendices
St Pol	20/8/17		Inspection of billets and lines of 9th H.H. at Ostreville, & inspection of Messes Nos 1, 2, 4 Signals officers & billets of P.B. men & Signals at Heuchin. 1. 1-8 seat latrine (bucket) for No 1 Mess. Monchy Cav cav. 2. 2-4 seat latrines for officers, & 2-4 trap latrines for Deccan Horse.	
	21/8/17		Inspection of Supply Col billets, bivouacs & kitchens &c at St Pol.	
	22/8/17		Roellecourt. 1 latrine for Aml. Bgde H.Q. & general cleaning work. 2 wells at billets - Nos 9 & 5-6 Ostreville tested & both good samples. Anvin. E.P.s.) water carts inspected. 1st D.G.s Ostreville) 34th P.H. 9th D.D.	
	23/8/17		Prouay. Conference ē D.D.M.S. Cav Corps re sanitation of Horse Show ground.	
	24/8/17		St Michel. Billets of 8th Hussars inspected. Work on manure dumps & drain put in for B squadron billet.	
	25/8/17		St Pol. 8 men for work at Havert. St Michel. General cleaning work for 8th Huss. Prouay. Work on Horse Show grounds.	

J. Mackem
Cpl. B.Pol.
for OC 5th (Cav) San Sect

WAR DIARY
or
INTELLIGENCE SUMMARY
(Erase heading not required.)

Army Form C. 2118

Place	Date	Hour	Summary of Events and Information	Remarks and references to Appendices
St Pol	26/8/17		Pronay. Work on Horse Show Ground. St Pol. 6 men for work at Harvest. Workshop. Structures & fittings, notices etc.	
"	27/8/17		" " " " " Pronay. Horse Show Ground.	
"	28/8/17		" " " " " Workshop. 1-1. Seat Latrine & Structure. Notice Boards. Pen pits for dust	
"	29/8/17		" 1-4 Seat D.P. Latrine. Pronay. Horse Show Ground.	
"	30/8/17		Henchin 1-1. Seat Latrine & Structure for L.A.M.B. &c. Pronay. Horse Show Ground. Workshop Notices. Paint & Ind for Horse Show. Handed over charge of Unit to Capt. Rythee I.M.S.	
"	31/8/17		Took over charge – Party for Horse Show grounds. Rythee Capt. I.M.S. O.C. No 5 (Cav.) San. Section	J.A. MacLean Capt. R.A.M.C.

Sept. 1917

5th Cav. Div. Sanitary Section.

COMMITTEE FOR THE
MEDICAL HISTORY OF THE WAR
Date   12 DEC. 1917

"Medical"

Serial No. 297

Army Form C. 2118

WAR DIARY
or
INTELLIGENCE SUMMARY

(Erase heading not required.)

No 5 (Cav.) Sanitary Section

Instructions regarding War Diaries and Intelligence Summaries are contained in F. S. Regs., Part II. and the Staff Manual respectively. Title Pages will be prepared in manuscript.

Place	Date	Hour	Summary of Events and Information	Remarks and references to Appendices
ST POL	1st Sep. 1917		Cav. Corps Horse Show near PRONAY — Total of 14 latrines, 4 urinals (trough), and a grease trap + sullage pit were made + screened for above.	
"	2nd		Party clearing Horse Show grounds + dismantling sanitary structures.	
"	3rd		Party at MARQUAY (9th Hodson's Horse). a 4-trap squat latrine completed. 2 old latrines closed. Foden disinfected huts for 3rd Garrison Guard Coy, ST POL	
"	4th + 5th		Party at MARQUAY made incinerator, urinals etc. Inspected billets etc at EPS-HERBEVAL (34th Horse) Foden at EPS worked for 34th Horse. Party at ST MICHEL, fitting latrines for 8th Hussars.	
"	6th		Foden at HERNICT for R. Can. Drags. Party at ST MICHEL, commenced drain for surface water. old manure dump covered. MARQUAY finished — Inspected 9th Horse billets etc at OSTREVILLE	
"	7th		OSTREVILLE — 2 squat latrines completed. ST MICHEL — drainage work finished.	
"	8th		OSTREVILLE cont. old latrines closed etc.. EPS-HERBEVAL — 2 latrines completed, incinerator built, wells tested. FODEN at ROELLECT. for 18th Lancers.	
"	9th		Sunday routine — medical inspection; box respirator inspection + drill; bathing + washing clothes	
"	10th		OSTREVILLE — an Indian (squat) latrines completed; old latrines closed. EPS-HERBEVAL — 2 latrines completed etc. Foden worked for 7th Can. F.A., 104th I.C. F.A. and Sanitary Section. Water tested + notices erected.	
"	11th		Party at HESTRUS (N Battery) water tested; latrines, urinals, grease-traps + sullage pits completed. Party at ROELLECT. erected latrine for Ambala Brig. H.Q. Amm. Col. lines inspected.	
"	12th		Party at LATHIEULOYE (Amm. Col.) built corr. iron incinerator.	

P.H. Lee
Capt. R.A.M.C.

WAR DIARY
or
INTELLIGENCE SUMMARY.

Army Form C. 2118

Instructions regarding War Diaries and Intelligence Summaries are contained in F. S. Regs., Part II. and the Staff Manual respectively. Title pages will be prepared in manuscript.

N° 5 (Cav) Sanitary Section

(Erase heading not required.)

Place	Date	Hour	Summary of Events and Information	Remarks and references to Appendices
ST POL	13th Sep. 1917		Party to Suffly Col. (ST POL) 2 latrines fitted + rubbish cleared. Party at L'ABBAYE DE NEUVILLE FARM (X Battery) erected corr. iron incinerator. Foden disinfector worked for 8th Hussars, 14th M.G.S. and 5th Reserve Park.	
"	14th		Work at HESTRUS (N Batt.) completed, incinerator + Indian latrine fitted; manure concentrated. Inspected billets etc. of Fort Garry Horse at BELVAL – ST MARTIN etc.	
"	15th		Party at OSTREVILLE new pits dug for latrines (22 seats). Foden worked for 34th Horse, 20th Horse, 7th Dr. Gds., and 13th M.G.S.	
"	16th		Sunday routine – Foden worked for Ld. Strathcona's H. and 141st I.C.F.A.	
"	17th		Party at LATHIEULOYE (Divl. Ammn. Col.) filled old latrines + rubbish pits; completed latrines sullage pits etc. Tested and marked three wells. Foden worked for 7th Drag. Gds. at ANVIN.	
"	18th		Party at MARQUAY, closed old latrines + dug new pits: OSTREVILLE, squat latrine completed. Foden at HEUCHIN, works for Div. H.Q. and 17th Brig. R.H.A. H.Q.	
"	19th		Party at HEUCHIN, closed old latrine + dug new pit; completed latrine for N° 4 Mess. Party at BERGNEUSE completed latrines for 17th Bn. R.H.A. H.Q., and attached signallers. Foden worked for 5th Res. Park and 9th Hodson's H. Under orders of A.D.M.S. 5th Cav. Div. took over additional medical charge of 5th Divl. Supply Column and Ammunition Park.	

R.H.Lee
Capt. A.M.S.

WAR DIARY or INTELLIGENCE SUMMARY

Army Form C. 2118

No 5 (Cav.) Sanitary Section

Place	Date	Hour	Summary of Events and Information	Remarks and references to Appendices
ST POL	20th Sept 1914		Party at ST POL (Supply Col.) erected two urinals with pits, dug new latrine pit + general scavenging. Foden worked for 104th I.C.F.A. and Fort Garry Horse. Inspected R.O.D. at HERVICT + PIERREMT.	
"	21st		Supply Col. cont. new latrine pits + urinals etc. — Workshop making an experimental Indian pattern pail latrine. Camp incinerator rebuilt to burn faeces. Refuse removed from Communal College. Party at HERNICOURT — new latrine pit dug + latrine erected.	
"	22nd		ST POL — 2 urinals + pits and new latrine pit for Supp. Col. + Amm. Park. Party at HERNICT. 2 — 4 seat latrines completed. Foden, weekly overhaul.	
"	23rd		Sunday routine — Med. Inspection; box respirator insp. + drill. Foden = XX Deacon House.	
"	24th		ST POL (Supp. Col. + Amm Park) urinals + new latrine pit dug. Foden disinfected all cast clothing of Ambala Brig. and Divl Troops: This will be done every Monday in future.	
"	25th		2 urinals for 101st I.C.F.A. New bench made for Workshop.	
"	26th		Party at HERNICOURT, screening 2 public latrines, + erecting urinal complete.	
"	27th		Party at BRYAS, screening 2 public latrines, repairing same + digging new latrine pit. Foden disinfected all cast clothing of Sec bad + Canadian Cav. Brigades + will do so every Thursday at WAVRANS.	
"	28th		ST POL — urinal completed + general cleaning of Garrison Guard camp. Inspected 7th D.O.3 at AVVIN.	
"	29th		Inspected A Squadron L.S. Horse at VAL HUON — urinals + latrines of Supp. Col. + Garrison Guards camp at ST POL sprayed cresol; general scavenging. Wire fencing of San. Sect. camp repaired.	
"	30th		Sunday routine — San. Sect. inspections — weekly overhaul Foden.	

R.H.Lee Capt. R.A.S.
O.C. No 5 (Cav.) Sanitary Section

Section

5th Cav. Sanitary Section.

COMMITTEE FOR THE
MEDICAL HISTORY OF THE WAR
Date -8 FEB. 1918

Medical

WAR DIARY or INTELLIGENCE SUMMARY

(Erase heading not required.)

Army Form C.2118

No 5 (Cav.) Sanitary Section

297

Place	Date	Hour	Summary of Events and Information	Remarks and references to Appendices
St POL	1st Oct 1917		Party completed trough urinal for Suffy Col. Foden = Ambala Brig. + Div. Troops cast clothing etc	
"	2nd		Party to MONCHY-CAYEUX, Indian pattern latrines fitted (11 seats), ditch cleared, and billets inspected (20th Deccan Horse). Foden worked for 14th M.G.S.	
"	4th		St POL, Garrison Guard Camp, sullage-water filter fitted to bath-house. Party to ROELLECOURT (18th Lancers) latrine pits dug + latrines fitted. Foden = Sec'bad Bn. + Can. Bn. cast clothing.	
"	5th		Party to MONCHY-CAYEUX (Sec'bad Bn. H.Q.) general scavenging. ROELLECT. latrines completed (18th Lancers). Foden worked for Royal Can. Dragoons.	
Camp south of STEENBECQUE Station	6th		Unit moved to camp south of STEENBECQUE with three lorries borrowed from Suffy Column.	
"	7th		Halt, work in camp and for Suffy Column camp.	
WATOU	8th		Unit moved to WATOU.	
"	9th		Work in WATOU; 10 sweepers scavenging the town (under Town Major's orders: to be continued daily) Town plan obtained from area San. Section (No 58) water from W. Points in town tested. Party to POPERINGHE to clean up No 1 Mess and fitted latrine, with roof. Party cleaned up area of 20th Deccan Horse (near WATOU). Inspected camp of Amm. Park and Can. Section Suffy Column at WINNAZEELE.	
"	10th		4 latrine pits dug and structures re-erected: 2 grease traps + sullage pits made: and 5 water sources tested in WATOU. Bivouacs of 34th P.H. and 20th D.H. inspected.	
"	11th		In WATOU latrine pit dug. 20th D.H. area scavenged. Inspected bivouacs of 7th D.G's. 13th + 14th M.G.S. and 18th Lancers. Arranged for water supply from sterilising lorry of No 2 Water Tanks Coy.	

P.H.Lee Capt. R.M.S.

WAR DIARY
or
INTELLIGENCE SUMMARY

Army Form C. 2118

Instructions regarding War Diaries and Intelligence Summaries are contained in F. S. Regs., Part II. and the Staff Manual respectively. Title Pages will be prepared in manuscript.

No 5 (Cav.) *(Erase heading not required.)* Sanitary Section

Place	Date	Hour	Summary of Events and Information	Remarks and references to Appendices
WATOU	12th Oct. 1917		Inspected bivouacs of 9th H.H. and N Battery. Bathing parade, army baths near WATOU. Foden disinfector worked for Supply Col. + Amm. Park.	
"	13th		Cleaned out filter of Army Baths at WATOU, refilling with new brick + concrete rubble, cleaned out soak pits. Dug new latrine pits for Ambala Br. H.Q. and erected complete latrine for 104th I.C.F.A.	
"	14th		2 5-seat latrines complete for 13th M.G.S.	
LEAUWETTE	15th		Unit moved LEAUWETTE (LUMBRES)	
"	16th		Halt.	
LA LOGE	17th		Unit moved to LALOGE. Party to FRESSIN (Div. H.Q.) scavenging + digging temporary latrines	
"	18th		FRESSIN continued - more latrines dug; latrine at No 1 mess re-erected on fresh site. Instructions of A.D.M.S. taken re absence of permanent latrines in present area. At LALOGE temporary latrines dug, water tests made and notices erected. 1 Br. N.C.O. and 4 sweepers temp. detached with "5th Cavalry Battn"	
"	19th		FRESSIN cont. - urinals made - water tested; incinerator rebuilt and fired, etc. Regtal M. Officers seen re sanitary requirements of their units. Party at PLANQUES, dug temp. latrines + cleaned up area.	
"	20th		Rough survey of Divl area continued: practically no sanitary structures exist. An estimate of latrines required by the Divn sent to O.C. Field Squadron. At PLANQUES 4 water sources tested and 3 marked by notice boards.	
"	21st		Sunday routine - Medical Inspection of personnel, bathing etc.	

R.H. Lee Capt. R.A.M.S.

WAR DIARY or INTELLIGENCE SUMMARY.

Army Form C. 2118.

Nº 5 (Cav.) Sanitary Section

Place	Date	Hour	Summary of Events and Information	Remarks and references to Appendices
LA LOGE	22nd Oct. 1917		1 Br. N.C.O. + 5 Sweepers temp. detached at FRUGES, H.Q. Secobad Brigade. Party cleaning roads and ditches in LALOGE.	
"	23rd		Party at MARESQUEL (Ambala Brig. H.Q. and 8th Hussars) scavenging: rubbish pits dug. Foden at BEAURAINVILLE worked for 18th Lancers, 20th Horse, Can. M.G.S. + 104th I.C.F.A.	
"	24th		Work at MARESQUEL continued – Sullage pit + 3 seat latrine pit dug. Work in S.S. camp. Inspected sanitation of Sup. Col. (Can. Section) at WAMIN.	
"	25th		Party at BEAURAIN CHATEAU (8th Hussars) general scavenging. At LALOGE, latrine complete also sullage pit + grease-trap: routine work in work-shop. 11 notice boards in MARENLA (L.S.H.) FODEN at BELLEVUE (F.G. Horse, 7th D.G., 13th M.G.S., Res. Park, Amm. Col. 34th Horse)	
"	26th		Party dug new latrines for Supply Column at LALOGE	
"	27th		Incinerator built at LALOGE; 8 urinals made in workshop. Foden at LALOGE (9th Horse, 14th M.G.S., 104th I.C.F.A., A.H.T.)	
"	28th		Party completed BEAURAIN CHATEAU (8th Hussars)	
"	29th		San. Section bathed at cotton factory in AUCHY-LES-HESDIN. Foden = L.S. Horse.	
"	30th		Party at WICQUINGHEM (A.H.T.) general scavenging, clearing ditches; corr. iron incinerator erected.	
"	31st		Party at FRESSIN (Div. H.Q.) altering urinal for Nº 1 Mess. Drawing empty petrol tins from HESDIN + delivering to Field Squadron at RENTY. Total of 160 seats squat latrines drawn from Field Squad. + delivered to Indian Units of Divn.	

R.H.Lee Capt. I.M.S.
O.C. Nº 5 (Cav.) Sanitary Section

Nov. 1917

5th Cav. Sanitary Section.

COMMITTEE FOR THE
MEDICAL HISTORY OF THE WAR
Date -8 FEB. 1918

Medical

WAR DIARY or INTELLIGENCE SUMMARY.

Army Form C. 2118.

No 5 (Cav.) Sanitary Section

Place	Date	Hour	Summary of Events and Information	Remarks and references to Appendices
LA LOGE	1st Nov. 1917		New pits for officers' latrines + urinals at LALOGE (Supply Col.) also cleaning + repairing roads. Notice boards painted + distributed to 9th Horse, 18th Lancers, + 104th I.C.F.A. Foden disinfected 1208 articles for R.C.H.A., R. Can. Dr., F.G. Horse, 34th Horse. 40 two-seater squat latrines distributed to Indian units	
"	2nd		Work at LALOGE as above. At FRUGES 5 water tests made; 30 notice boards erected. Billets and general sanitation inspected. Foden = Reserve Park. 38 two-seater squat latrines to Indian Units.	
"	3rd		New winch fitted to No 3 well at LALOGE. Iron incinerators and notice boards erected at MARENLA, EMBRY, and ERGNY. At FRUGES, inspection of billets etc of Amm. Park. Foden = Supply Col. and 13th M.G.S.	
"	4th + 5th		Parties repairing roads at LALOGE. Medical inspection of personnel; bathing parade at factory AUCHY-LES-HESDIN cotton factory.	
"	6th + 7th		Road repairing at LALOGE continued. Foden worked for 8th Hussars, 18th Lancers, Amb. Br. H.Q. 20th Horse, Aux. H. Transport, 141st I.C.F.A.	
"	8th		Party to AUBIN-ST VAAST (18th Lancers) general scavenging. Short course of instruction given to water duty men of Amm. Park, Amm. Col., Res. Park and N. Battery R.H.A. Prepared plan of sanitation of LALOGE - WAMIN. Foden = F.G. Horse, 7th D.Gs, Amm. Park, Res. Park, + Amm. Col.	
"	9th + 10th		Scavenging LALOGE - WAMIN, evacuated by Supply Column.	

R H Lee
Capt. I.M.S.

WAR DIARY or INTELLIGENCE SUMMARY.

Army Form C. 2118.

No. 5 (Cav.) Sanitary Section

Place	Date	Hour	Summary of Events and Information	Remarks and references to Appendices
QUINCONCE (PERONNE)	11th Nov. 1917		Unit moved to camp at QUINCONCE by lorries lent by 5th Cav. Supply Col.	
"	12th		Party for fatigue work at LA CHAPELLETTE under R.S.O. 4 seat squat latrine completed. Old latrines closed + incinerator repaired at QUINCONCE.	
"	13th		Party for R.S.O. as above (making ration dump). Work in camp, sullage pits etc.	
"	14th		Party for R.S.O. 12 latrine seats completed with pits for Supply Col. 2 water carts of Supply Col. inspected. 1 N.C.O. + 8 sweepers temp. detached at BOUVINCOURT, Div. H.Q.	
"	15th		Fatigue party for R.S.O. 1 heating stove and 1 corr. iron incinerator made for Supply Col.	
"	16th		Party to BRUSLE, (18th Lancers) general scavenging + channeling roads. Capt. R.H. LEE R.A.M.S. assumed additional medical charge of Res. Park at FLAMICOURT.	
"	17th		Res. Park water cart inspected + deficiencies reported to O.C. Billets + lines in good condition. Detachment at Div. H.Q. have done general cleaning up, concentrated + covered manure, made 7 grease-traps + sullage pits, + fitted one 2 seat squat latrine.	
"	18th		Detachment rejoined from BOUVINCOURT. Detachment rejoined from 5th Cavalry Battalion. Work at BRUSLE continued. Med. Insp. + bathing of personnel.	
"	19th		Work at BRUSLE completed. Party dug field latrines near Dessart Wood near FINS	
"	20th + 21st		Party at BOUVINCOURT cleaned vacated billet of Div. H.Q. + disposed of refuse; also at VRAIGNES (13th M.G.S.) this area being occupied by French troops.	

R.H. Lee
Capt. R.A.M.S.

WAR DIARY or INTELLIGENCE SUMMARY

Army Form C. 2118.

No 5 (Cav.) Sanitary Section

Place	Date	Hour	Summary of Events and Information	Remarks and references to Appendices
QUINCONCE (PERONNE)	22nd Nov 1917		Party in PERONNE road cleaning. Party at BOUCLY cleaned up A.H. Transport + Res. Park area and completed 6 seater latrine.	
"	23rd		Party at BOUCLY cleaned up area of B Echelons of Divn + burnt refuse.	
PROYART	24th		Unit moved to PROYART.	
"	25th		Party to SUZANNE (Div. H.Q.) cleaning billets + offices in Chateau. Inspected Sanitation of PROYART + tested four water sources.	
"	26th		SUZANNE continued – lines of Can. M.G.S. and Can. Bde. H.Q. cleaned up.	
"	27th		At PROYART, 2 - 4 seater latrines completed for Suppy Col. Party detached to MONCHY-LAGACHE (new Div. H.Q.) cleaned 15 Bow Huts + 2 barns. Work for No 1 Mess.	
MONCHY-LAGACHE	28th		Unit moved to MONCHY-LAGACHE – four 1 seat officers latrines completed. Stoves fitted for No 1 Mess + G.O.C. + brick paths made between mess and officers huts. Capt R.H. LEE I.M.S. relinquished medical charge of 5th Cav. Suppy Column.	
"	29th		At Div. H.Q. 3 urinals completed, 1 closed brick incinerator built, Manure Dump marked + various sanitary notice boards fixed. Party at TERTRY – 6 seater latrines fixed. At CAUVIGNY FARM an open brick incinerator built, a six seat latrine fitted + general scavenging.	
"	30th		At MONCHY 6 seater latrine fixed, also 1 officer's latrine. Party at TERTRY – general scavenging	

R.H. Lee
Capt. I.M.S.
O.C. No 5 (Cav.) Sanitary Section

Dec. 1917.

5th Cav. San. Sect.

Medical

WAR DIARY
or
INTELLIGENCE SUMMARY.

Army Form C. 2118.
(297)

Nº 5 (Cav.) Sanitary Section

December 1917

Place	Date	Hour	Summary of Events and Information	Remarks and references to Appendices
ATHIES	1st Dec. 1917		Unit moved to ATHIES. Arrangements made to act as rest for temp. medical charge of B echelons + details of the Divn. in ATHIES area. One two seat latrine completed.	
"	2nd		Inspection of billets etc. of all 5th Cav. units + details in ATHIES area. 2 N.C.O.s + 24 sweepers temp. detached to Div. H.Q. at E.5.a for scavenging.	
V.8 central (to.ooo 62c)	3rd		Unit moved to camp at V.8 central (Map 40,000 62c). Party detached on 2nd inst. rejoined.	
"	4th		2 two-seat + 1 one-seat officers latrines; and 10 two seat men's latrines fitted near camp V.8 central for reinforcements etc. of the Divn. Part of unit being quartered in horse lines these were improved by sedge shelters for walls etc.	
"	5th		Work improving camp. Party cleaned up lines evacuated by Res. Park at DEVISE	
"	6th + 7th		Seven 2-seat latrines completed + fitted for Divn. Reinf. etc, and general scavenging	
"	8th + 9th		Clearing manure from standing etc, in ATHIES	
"	10th + 11th		Party to MONCHY-LAGACHE to clean up area to be occupied by D.H.Q. Rubbish burnt.	
"	12th to 14th		Parties to BRUSLE and CARTIGNY cleaning up area occupied by Ambala Brigade. Foden worked for San.Sect. & Divn. Reinforcements.	
"	15th		Iron incinerator fitted for Divn. Reinf. Camp. Foden worked for Amm. Col. 17th Brig. Party to camp north of DEVISE cleaning 34th Poona Horse lines huts etc: latrine pit dug.	
"	16th		DEVISE continued, iron incinerator erected. Party to MONCHY-LAGACHE cleaned billets vac. by French troops. Foden worked for Cav. R.H.A. Amm. Col. + Res. Park.	
"	17th		Unit moved to MONCHY-LAGACHE — was relieved of med. charge of Divn. Reinf., Res. Park, Amm. Cols.	

RHLee
Capt I.M.S.

WAR DIARY or INTELLIGENCE SUMMARY.

N⁰ 5 (Cav.) Sanitary Section

Army Form C. 2118.

Place	Date	Hour	Summary of Events and Information	Remarks and references to Appendices
MONCHY -LAGACHE	18th Dec. 1917		Inspected billets + water carts at MONCHY-LAGACHE (Div. H.Q.; Res. Park, and Amm. Col⁰), party cleaning huts + billets. Foden at disposal of Cav. Brigade.	
"	19th		Party clearing D.A.D.O.S. stores, snow etc. Sanford motor water tank inspected + water sources in MONCHY tested. Foden = Cav Brigade.	
"	20th		Latrines fitted for Sec'bad M.V.S. at MONCHY, ditto for F.P.O. N⁰ 40. Foden = D.A.D.O.S.	
"	21st		Party at MONCHY for general scavenging of village. Foden = Cav. Brigade.	
"	22nd		Fitted small bath-house at MONCHY for Amm. Col⁰ + Res. Park; fatigue party assisted repair of an Adrian hut. Latrines fitted for Res. Park + Signals officers' mess.	
"	23rd		Sunday routine, inspection of unit, bathing etc. Foden detached for work with 3rd Cav. Div⁰ at POEUILLY.	
"	24th		At MONCHY latrines fitted for French Mission and Civil Population + nec. notices.	
"	25th		Christmas day - a holiday.	
"	26th		Alterations to a Bow Hut for A.D.V.S. Completed 4 seat latrine for civil population	
"	27th		Levelling floor + disinfecting Adrian hut for Div. Canteen. Inspected A.H.T. lines at ESTREE-en-CH.	
"	28th		Party to TERTRY fitting latrines + urinal for Amb. Brig. H.Q., + digging grave for civilian.	
"	29th		Completed latrine for W.O. Div. H.Q. filled in old latrines etc. Foden returned from 3rd Cav. Div⁰	
"	30th		Party to POEUILLY fitting latrines for 5th Cav. Lian. Party + inspected billets. Inspection of Cav. Cav. Br. re manure disposal + latrines.	
"	31st		Buried horse at MONCHY. Marking manure dumps near MONTECOURT + MEREAUCOURT for Cav. Brigade. Foden = cart clothing disinfected for D.A.D.O.S.	

R.H. Lee Capt/MS
O.C. N⁰ 5 (Cav) San. Section

Medical

WAR DIARY *or* **INTELLIGENCE SUMMARY.**
(Erase heading not required.)

No 5 (Cav) Sanitary Section

January 1918.

Army Form C. 2118.

297

Place	Date	Hour	Summary of Events and Information	Remarks and references to Appendices
MONCHY -LAGACHE	1st Jan. 1918		Work in camp. Foden at TERTRY worked for 8th Hussars.	
"	2nd		Party at MERAUCOURT fixed officers latrines for Can. Brig. H.Q. 14 latrine + manure dump notices erected for Can. Brig.	
"	3rd		Inspected 5th Cav. Dism. Reinforcement camp at POEUILLY and erected latrine + incinerator. Re-erected officers latrine for Amb. Brig. H.Q. at TERTRY. Foden at TREFCON for 34th Horse.	
"	4th		Party at CAUVIGNY FARM erected 2 four-seat latrines for 14th M.G.S. and an incinerator for 8th Hussars. At MERAUCOURT - MONTECOURT 2-4 seat and 5-2 seat latrines completed for R.C.D. + F.G. Horse. Foden = 34th Horse	
"	5th		Took over supervision of TERTRY, TREFCON and CAULAINCOURT areas from No 59 Sanitary Section. Inspected Div. H.Q. messes, cook-houses, billets etc. with D.A.D.M.S. 5th Cav. Div. Completed 2 trough urinals and sullage pit. Party at TREFCON dug 2-8 seat latrine pits, fitted 3 grease traps + sullage pits for Sec'd Brig. H.Q. Foden at TREFCON worked for 20th Horse.	
"	6th		Sunday - Gas respirator drill + inspection. All kits of personnel Fodened.	
"	7th		Party at TREFCON dug latrine pits + completed corr. iron incinerator for 7th D.G. Foden disinfected 1020 articles cast clothing for D.A.D.O.S.	
"	8th		Inspected camps of Seabad Brigade troops at TREFCON: notice boards erected. At MONCHY-LAGACHE, Signal officer's latrine + grease trap + sullage pit completed. At MONTECOURT one 3 seat latrine completed for R.C.D. Foden at TREFCON worked for 20th Horse. Inspected camps of 18th Lancers + 8th Hussars.	
"	9th		Screen + roof erected for W.O.'s latrine at Div. H.Q. Inspected camp of 9th Hodson's Horse. Party at TERTRY removed manure from Amb. Brig. H.Q. to dump. Party at TREFCON dug new latrine pits + screened latrines. Foden worked for 141st I.C.F.A.	
"	10th		Inspection of A + B Batteries (R.C.H.A.) wagon lines, + fitted two 2-seater latrines. Work in camp assembling corr. iron incinerators and making urinals.	

RF Lee Capt/RMS

WAR DIARY or INTELLIGENCE SUMMARY

Army Form C. 2118.

N° 5 (Cav.) Sanitary Section

Place	Date	Hour	Summary of Events and Information	Remarks and references to Appendices
MONCHY-LAGACHE	11th Jan. 1918		Party at TREFCON fitted 6 trough urinals + an officer's latrine: at TERTRY fitted 5 urinals + 1 incinerator. At MONCHY made grease trap + sullage pit for Signals; also screened + cleaned two French cabinets.	
"	12th		At MONCHY dug new pit for 6 seat latrine + completed two 2-seaters. Inspected R.C.D. Foden = R.A.D.G. Sanitary area of section defined as follows:— Northern + Eastern boundaries:— Line from P.30d 3.7 through + inclusive of CAULAINCOURT to R. OMIGNON. Western Boundary:— line between 4th + 5th Cav. Divns (west of MONCHY-LAGACHE). Southern Boundary:— the line between Cavalry Corps + French Corps.	
"	13th		Iron incinerator erected for 9th Horse. Inspected L.S. Horse and 7th D.G.s esp. re manure disposal; also camp of 34th Labour Bn at TERTRY and Ambala Brig. Baths. Foden = 7th Can. Field Ambulance.	
"	14th		Iron incinerator erected for Divl Canteen at MONCHY. Inspected lines of Suff. Yeo. and aux. H.T. at ESTRÉES-EN-CHAUSSÉE. Inspected Water Points with pumping stations at TREFCON & CAULAINCOURT. Foden = D.A.D.O.S.	
"	15th		List of latrines + urinals in MONCHY-LAGACHE supplied to Area Comm. DEVISE. Party at TERTRY fitted trough urinal, 2 seater and one officer's latrine for Amb. Brig. Baths. Foden worked for 7th Drag. Gds.	
"	16th		Inspected camp of U Battery R.H.A. west of CAULAINCOURT. Work in camp on parapets for huts. Foden, D.A.D.O.S.	
"	17th		Party to MERAUCOURT scavenging Can. Brig. H.Q. and Ration Dump. At TREFCON fitted 10 "Manure Dump" + 2 "Water Points" notices, and 4 two-trap squat latrines for 34th Horse. Foden could not move (Thaw Scheme) but worked for D.A.D.O.S.	

R.H. Lee
Capt. R.A.M.S.

WAR DIARY or INTELLIGENCE SUMMARY

Army Form C. 2118

No 5 (Cav) Sanitary Section

Place	Date	Hour	Summary of Events and Information	Remarks and references to Appendices
MONCHY-LAGACHE	18th Jan. 1918		Party at MERAUCOURT scavenging Can. Brig. H.Q. and Ration Dump; ditto for 17th R.H.A. Amm. Col. Commenced short course of field Sanitation for Capt. McCullagh C.A.M.C. Inspected lines of 20th Horse.	
"	19th		Visited School of Sanitation (Peronne) with Capt. McCullagh. Condemned water cart of R.C.H.A. Amm. Col. Three 2-seat latrines fitted for 17th Brig. R.H.A. Amm. Col.	
"	20th		Inspected all Can. Brig. Manure Dumps and interviewed O.C. units re manure disposal, explaining current orders. Fitted a filter-box and dug soak pit for sullage water from Ambala Brig. Baths at TERTRY.	
"	21st		Party scavenging MONCHY-LAGACHE. Interviewed Brig. General Canadian Brig. re manure disposal. Party at TERTRY covering old manure dump + digging 2 latrine pits. Foden = work for R.C.H.A.	
"	22nd		At TERTRY two latrines completed. One officer's latrine completed for Div. H.Q. Interviewed Area Commandant, DEVISE re manure dumps etc. Foden = F.G. Horse.	
"	23rd		Party on Manure Dump, MONCHY-LAGACHE. Interviewed O.C. all units in MONCHY re manure disposal, explaining orders. Units represent that tons of manure were found near stables and standing when this Divn moved into this area: a great deal of this has been removed. Foden = F.G. Horse.	
"	24th		Party at MONCHY fitted new latrine for Div. H.Q. Messes, dug new pit for public latrine, and worked on manure dump, LANCHY Road. Party assisted 14th M.G.S. with manure disposal at CAUVIGNY farm. Inspected lines of 5th Field Squadron + 13th M.G.S. Foden = D.A.D.O.S.	

R.H.Lee
Capt. AVS

WAR DIARY or INTELLIGENCE SUMMARY

No 5 (Cav.) Sanitary Section

Army Form C. 2118.

Place	Date	Hour	Summary of Events and Information	Remarks and references to Appendices
MONCHY-LAGACHE	25th Jan 1918		Party cleaned up 13th M.G.S. camp - interviewed the O.C. re manure disposal. Party fitted one off. latrine + 2 urinals for 34th Horse, & one officers latrine for N Battery. Foden = R.C.H.A. Amm. Col. including horse rugs (sarcoptic mange). 4 men detached	Sec'ded Dis'm 1 Brigade
"	26th		Erected an iron incinerator for 13th M.G.S. Foden = 13th M.G.S. Completed new 6 seat public latrine for MONCHY - Interviewed O.C. 17th R.H.A. Amm. Col. R.Can. H.A. Amm. Col. and 5 Reserve Park re manure disposal. Interviewed O.C. 9th Sanitary Section re forward area to be taken over. 4 men	detached Ambala Dis'm Brigade.
"	27th		1 N.C.O. + 10 men temp. detached to VERMAND, and 1 N.C.O. ditto to BERNES to take over area as defined in A.D.M.S. No M/20/20 dated 27/1/18. Boundaries :- Northern Boundary - line through + exclusive of VRAIGNES, FLECHIN, VENDELLES, JEANCOURT, VILLERET. Western Boundary - line from P.30 d 3.7 (Map 62c 1/40000) through + exclusive of CAULAINCOURT to R. OMIGNON - Southern Boundary - The river OMIGNON. This area is additional to that already held, vide, this diary of 12th Jan. 1918. 1 N.C.O. and 10 men temp. detached at BOUVINCOURT to be under the direct orders of A.D.M.S. Dismounted Divisions - Remainder of Section, scavenging area at MONCHY evacuated by H.Q. 5th Cav. Div. Foden = 9th Horse.	

R.H. Lee
Capt. I.M.S.

WAR DIARY or INTELLIGENCE SUMMARY

Army Form C. 2118.

No 5 (Cav.) Sanitary Section

Place	Date	Hour	Summary of Events and Information	Remarks and references to Appendices
MONCHY-LAGACHE	28th Jan. 1918		Party cleaned up vacated lines of Can. Brig. H.Q. + R. Can. Dragoons, and vacated billets of 5th Cav. Div. H.Q. Also filled in old latrine. Inspected water suppy of LE VERGUIER and reported to "Q" Dism. Divisions. Interviewed A.C. VENDELLES re conditions in his area. Foden = 9th Horse.	
"	29th		Party cleaning up area vacated by Can. Brigade. Inspected VERMAND, billets, baths etc, and baths at VADENCOURT, and report submitted to A.D.M.S. Dismounted Divisions.	
"	30th		Party cleaning up TERTRY and area vacated by AMBALA Brigade. Handed over the whole area held by this unit to No 12. Sanitary Section, 3rd Cav. Divn.	
DOMART-EN-PONTHIEU	31st		1 N.C.O. and 10 men temp. detached at VERMAND and 1 N.C.O. at BERNES were withdrawn. The Section (less 1 N.C.O. and 10 men detached at BOUVINCOURT) (and 8 men detached with Sec'bad & Ambala Dist Brigades.) moved to Back area billets at DOMART-EN-PONTHIEU.	

R.P.H.
Capt. R.A.M.S.
O.C. No 5 (Cav.) Sanitary Section

Aug 1918.

Can Div
No. 5 San. Sect.

COMMITTEE
MEDICAL HIST
Date 23 AUG 1918

WAR DIARY or **INTELLIGENCE SUMMARY.**

No 5 (Cav.) Sanitary Section

Army Form C. 2118.

Place	Date	Hour	Summary of Events and Information	Remarks and references to Appendices
Troop train M.E.D. No 696 H.V.S	1st March 1918 to 3rd		Travelling – San. Sect. Two men developed symptoms of mumps on evening of 3/3/18. After consultation with O.C. train at Sta. GAZALY I.M.S. it was decided to take them on in the train.	R6
"	4th		San Sect. One man with diarrhoea & fever (mumps contact) evacuated sick at VINTIMILLE.	R6
"	5th		The two mumps cases above were admitted to Hospital at FAENZA.	R6
"	6th to 8th		Travelling – arrived CIMINO camp (TARANTO) on evening 8th.	R6
"	9th to 11th		Detrained & sent to rest camp.	R6
H.T. LEASOWE CASTLE	12th		Capt. R. H. LEE I.M.S. and one O.O.R. embarked at 16.30 hours on H.T. Leasowe Castle with the equipment of the unit. All the remaining Indian ranks (total 19) were detained in the rest camp as mumps contacts, according to orders of S.M.O. TARANTO. Capt. R. H. LEE took medical charge of troops on H.T. LEASOWE CASTLE.	
"	20th		Arrived ALEXANDRIA, reported to Emb. Medical Officer and handed over medical diary kept while on board.	
Camp TEL-EL-KEBIR	21st		Disembarked, entrained, detrained at TEL-EL-KEBIR and reached camp at 16.0 hours. Reported arrival at S.M.O. office.	
"	22nd		Reported to S.M.O. TEL-EL-KEBIR. Advanced party of 22 followers who left the unit on 23/1/18 rejoined. Interviewed O.C. No 29 San. Section who have charge of the camp area.	

R.H. Lee
Capt. I.M.S.

WAR DIARY
or
INTELLIGENCE SUMMARY

Army Form C. 2118.

No 5 (Cav) Sanitary Section

Place	Date	Hour	Summary of Events and Information	Remarks and references to Appendices
Camp TEL-EL-KEBIR	23rd March 1918		Accompanied O.C. 29th San. Section in making a Sanitary Inspection of part of the camp. Reported to "Q" adv. H.Q. 5th Cav. Divn. Box car, side-car & 1 B.O.R. A.S.C. M.T. rejoined.	
"	24th		Continued inspection of the camp with O.C. 29th S.S. reorganised latrine distribution of the 4th + 5th Cav. medical sector of the camp.	
"	25th		3 R.A.M.C. N.C.O.s and 31 followers of No 4 (Cav) Sanitary Section were temp. attached for duty. The personnel were allotted to the various camp sites occupied by the 11 Indian Cav. Regts of the 4th + 5th Cav. Divisions, also a veterinary hospital and the Indian Base Depot.	
"	26th		Routine work + inspection.	
"	27th		Ditto — Consulted Works Officer R.E. and O.C. 29th S.S. with ref. to fly-proofing latrine buckets, and sullage disposal of west end of camp (B camp).	
"	28th to 31st		Routine inspection of camps + lines occupied by various western cavalry units.	

R.H. Key
Capt. R.S.
O.C. No 5 (Cav) Sanitary Section

April 1915

No. 5 (Can) Gen. Hosp.

WAR DIARY or INTELLIGENCE SUMMARY

Army Form C. 2118.

(Erase heading not required.) **Sanitary Section**

Stamp: ARMY HEAD QUARTERS INDIA, 28 MAY 1918, MEDICAL BRANCH — No 5 Cav.

Place	Date	Hour	Summary of Events and Information	Remarks and references to Appendices
Camp TEL-EL-KEBIR	1st April 1918		Routine inspection of lines of cavalry units in camp. Regimental sanitary details supplemented in units as necessary by San. Section personnel, either temp. detached or visiting units daily for duty at incinerators etc.	
"	2nd		2 sweepers temp. detached to 20th Deccan Horse, and 2 sweepers ditto to 38th C.I.H. for duty. Interview with Area Commandant re rubbish in site 6.	
"	3rd		Routine work & inspections in camp.	
"	4th		Took temp. command of No 29 San. Section during absence of O.C. on duty.	
"	5th		10 followers rejoined the unit of the 19 left at rest camp TARANTO.	
"	6th		Routine work & inspections: several pit urinals completed. Manure dump is now on canal bank.	
"	7th		Barges for manure not arrived, & manure accumulating. This matter is being reported by O.C. 29th San. Section. O.C.s of 29th L. 36th H. and Ind. Cav. Base Depot written to re accumulation of ashes at incinerators. Two mumps tents disinfected.	
"	8th		Div. H.Q. ablution shed, drains & sullage outfall cleaned. Two huts & one tent disinfected.	
"	9th		O.C. 19th Lancers & 9th Horse notified re fly-breeding in manure in their lines. 2 followers of 5th San. Sect. and 3 followers 4th San. Section proceeded on leave to India. Reported to S.M.O. camp that a large party of 36th Horse were bathing in an irrigation canal. 9 followers rejoined the unit (the balance of the party left at Rest Camp TARANTO.)	
"	10th		Usual routine work & inspections. A horse buried, 2 tents disinfected etc.	

R.H. Lee Capt. I.M.S.
O.C. No 5 (Cav.) Sanitary Section

WAR DIARY or ~~INTELLIGENCE SUMMARY~~

Army Form C. 2118.

No 5 (Cav.) Sanitary Section

Place	Date	Hour	Summary of Events and Information	Remarks and references to Appendices
Camp TEL-EL-KEBIR	11th April 1918		Routine work and inspections of area in camp occupied by cavalry and veterinary units.	
"	12th		S.M.O. again informed of men bathing in canal. Horse buried; mumps tents disinfected.	
"	13th + 14th		M.O. 29th Lancers asked to remove accumulation of manure near incinerators. The Admin. Commandant TEL-EL-KEBIR informed that manure is being dumped into the Sweet Water Canal by the men employed by manure contractor; also that milk is being sold in camp in very dirty bottles.	
"	15th + 16th		The lines 19th Lancers + 6th Cav. were vacated and cleaned up.	
"	17th		The vacated lines of 29th L. and 36th H. were cleaned up.	
"	18th		2 sweepers temp. detached 20th Deccan Horse rejoined.	
"	19th to 22nd		Routine inspections, and clearing camp sites vacated by cavalry units.	
"	23rd		On arrival of O.C. No 4 (Cav) Sanitary Section the details of that unit temp. attached to No 5 (Cav.) Sanitary Section rejoined their own unit.	
"	24th		In accordance with A.D.M.S. 5th Cav. Div: No 1062/18 dated 24/4/18 deficiencies of No 4 (Cav.) San. Section in personnel, transport and equipment were made good from No 5 (Cav.) San. Section i.e. 13 followers were transferred. Also Douglas side-car combination + miscellaneous tools and stores. Major R.H. LEE I.M.S. handed over command of the unit to Major R.C. O'BRIEN I.M.S. RHLee Major IMS.	

WAR DIARY
or
INTELLIGENCE SUMMARY

Army Form C. 2118.

No 5 (Cav.) Sanitary Section

Place	Date	Hour	Summary of Events and Information	Remarks and references to Appendices
CAMP TEL-EL-KEBIR	27/4/18		2 sweepers were transferred to Sec'bad I.C.F.A. and one sweeper transferred from Sec'bad I.C.F.A. 8 sweepers were sent to No 137 Stationary Hospital to be temporarily attached to that unit.	
"	28/4/18		Major R.H. LEE I.M.S. rejoined the unit.	
"	29/4/18		L/Cpl. Mach, No 054976, A.S.C.(M.T.) was ordered to report to Sec'bad I.C.F.A. to be attached to that unit.	
"	30/4/18		1 B.O.R. reported from H.Q. 5th Cav. Div= for duty as batman. Note - The effective strength of the unit now is Bri. O. 1 Bri. O.R. 2 I.O.R. 14 (S. + 2 Followers) Total 17	

R.H. Lee
Major I.M.S.
O.C. No 5 (Cav.) Sanitary Section

www.ingramcontent.com/pod-product-compliance
Lightning Source LLC
Chambersburg PA
CBHW081239170426
43191CB00034B/1981